THE LOUISIANA CEMETERY HANDBOOK

This book is a guide for interested notaries, attorneys, funeral directors, church officials, and cemetery directors. It is not legal advice nor the practice of law. The author draws on his practical experience in the field as a cemetery director and as a commissioned Louisiana Civil Law Notary Public, but does not hold himself out to be an attorney at law. Those using any suggestions and forms are advised to confirm and update them with their own research. Use of this book constitutes full and voluntary acceptance of the risk of error, misapplication, or invalidity.

Any statement of "should" or "is advised" or similar is based on the author's personal and practical experience. It is not legal advice.

THE LOUISIANA CEMETERY HANDBOOK

Law, Compliance, and Administration

A comprehensive guide to Louisiana cemetery law, Title 8 statutes, case law, and regulatory compliance.

JOSHUA R. LEBLANC

Bayou State PUBLISHING

For permission requests, contact:
Bayou State Publishing
P.O. Box 1049
Abbeville, LA 70511
Email: info@bayoustatepublishing.com
Website: bayoustatepublishing.com

ISBN: 978-1-970659-00-9

Printed in the United States of America
First Edition, 2025

Published by **Bayou State Publishing**
Youngsville, LA

Disclaimer:
The information contained in this book is provided for general educational and informational purposes only. Nothing in this book should be construed as, or relied upon as, legal advice. Laws and regulations vary by jurisdiction and are subject to change. Readers are strongly encouraged to consult with a qualified attorney before making any decisions or taking any action based on the material presented herein. The author and publisher expressly disclaim any liability for actions taken or not taken based on the contents of this book.

ABOUT THE AUTHOR

Joshua R. LeBlanc serves as the Executive Director of Holy Family Cemetery in New Iberia, Louisiana. He was ordained a Catholic deacon for the Diocese of Lafayette in 2016 and is currently assigned to St. Martin de Tours Catholic Church in St. Martinville.

Deacon LeBlanc brings a unique combination of theological insight, pastoral care, and administrative precision to the sacred work of cemetery management.

He holds a Master of Arts in Moral Theology and a +30 in Bioethics from Holy Apostles College and Seminary and is certified in Bioethics by the National Catholic Bioethics Center. He is currently pursuing a Doctorate in the field of Bioethics.

In addition to his ministry and administrative leadership, Deacon LeBlanc is a commissioned Civil Law Notary Public in and for the State of Louisiana and the owner of two small businesses – an IT firm and Chesterton's Fine Cigars in Youngsville, La. It is through this background that he shares his expertise in faith, ethics, and cemetery law.

Deacon LeBlanc also serves as a police chaplain and reserve police officer for the Youngsville and Abbeville Police Departments. He is also chaplain for the Military and Hospitaller Order of St. Lazarus of Jerusalem in the rank of Ecclesiastical Commander, whose mission is to serve the sick and dying. He is the Delegate for the Imperial Calcasieu Delegation and Vice Chancellor for Communications for the Grand Priory of America

As a deacon, he has ministered to grieving families for years, guiding them through the Catholic Church's teachings on death, burial, and resurrection. As a professional cemetery administrator, he has developed robust compliance systems rooted in Louisiana law, ensuring that every interment, fund, and record upholds both the dignity of the deceased and the legal obligations of the living.

Deacon LeBlanc is the author of *The Louisiana Cemetery Form Book: Legal Documents, Templates, and Compliance Tools for Cemetery Authorities and Notaries Public*, the companion book in this series. Together, these works form the foundation of *The Louisiana Cemetery Authority Series*, a comprehensive legal and operational reference for religious and civil cemetery professionals throughout the state.

He and his wife, Annie, reside in Abbeville, Louisiana, with their cat Benedict.

THE LOUISIANA CEMETERY AUTHORITY SERIES

The Louisiana Cemetery Handbook: Law, Compliance, and Administration: A comprehensive guide to Louisiana cemetery law, Title 8 statutes, case law, and regulatory compliance.

The Louisiana Cemetery Forms Book: Documents, Templates, and Compliance Tools for Cemetery Authorities and Notaries Public. A companion volume containing practical forms, sample contracts, affidavits, and checklists for daily operations.

Catholic and Cultural Burial Traditions in Louisiana: A Guide to Faith, Heritage, and Sacred Practice. A comprehensive exploration of Louisiana's Catholic, Cajun, Creole, African American, and Native burial customs, offering theological insight, cultural history, and practical guidance for cemetery professionals and families.

Louisiana Cemetery Case Law: Jurisprudence, Practical Lessons, and Title 8 in the Courts. A clear and practical guide to Louisiana's major cemetery cases, this volume explains how courts interpret Title 8 in real-world disputes involving burial authority, disinterment, family cemeteries, undeveloped land sales, trust funds, and historic burial protections.

The Notary's Guide to Louisiana Cemetery Law: Authority, Documentation, and Practice Under Title 8. A practical reference that equips Louisiana notaries with clear, compliant language, clauses, and pastoral guidance for navigating cemetery ownership, interment rights, and Title 8 obligations in everyday notarial practice.

THE COMPANION BOOK IN THIS SERIES

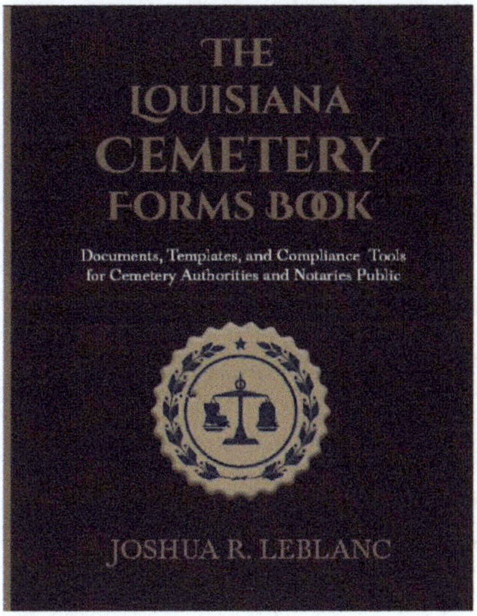

THE LOUISIANA CEMETERY FORMS BOOK

Documents, Templates, and Compliance Tools for Cemetery Authorities and Notaries Public.

The Louisiana Cemetery Handbook provides the legal framework, historical context, and best practices governing cemetery operation under Louisiana law. Yet, the actual work of compliance, administration, and family service is carried out through the forms, affidavits, and instruments that bring these principles to life.

Available through participating bookstores, Amazon.com, and editable Word Documents available at **LaCemeteryBook.com**

This indispensable companion volume includes:

- Fully formatted sample forms aligned with Title 8 and Louisiana Administrative Code requirements.
- Notarial templates for acts of sale, dation en paiement, affidavit of heirship, waiver of interment rights, exchange agreements, and more.
- Operational checklists and compliance tools for perpetual care reporting, merchandise funds, and burial recordkeeping.
- Editable Word versions for direct use by cemetery staff and notaries.
- Citations to the precise statutory and regulatory authorities governing each form.

Why You Need Both

Where the Handbook explains why the law exists, the Forms Book shows you how to apply it. Together, they form a complete, practical library for Louisiana's cemetery professionals, ensuring every interment, sale, and record is handled lawfully, ethically, and efficiently.

ACKNOWLEDGMENTS

To properly thank and acknowledge everyone who has played a part in this work is a monumental task – one I approach with both gratitude and trepidation, lest I inadvertently forget anyone.

First and foremost, my sincere thanks to Alan and Michele Childress, who have been mentors and friends since I first began my journey to become a civil law notary public. Their encouragement, guidance, and willingness to promote my work from its earliest stages have been invaluable. Thank you both for your steadfast support and belief in me.

I also wish to express my gratitude to Brother Brian Harrington, OSB. I spent four formative years at St. Joseph Seminary College in Covington, and now, more than twenty-five years later, I find myself still learning from the monks, this time in the sacred ministry of caring for the dead and their families. Thank you, Brother Brian, for your mentorship and for sharing the Benedictine tradition of reverence and care for the souls of the faithful departed at St. Joseph Abbey.

My heartfelt appreciation also extends to the two pastors of the parishes that own Holy Family Cemetery, where I have the privilege of serving.

Father William Blanda, a long-time friend who vested me as a deacon at my ordination, has been a constant source of support and encouragement. Father, thank you for your friendship through the years and for entrusting me with the opportunity to serve God's people as Executive Director of Holy Family Cemetery.

Father Garrett Savoie, another dear friend and even a groomsman at my wedding, could not have known that more than twenty years later he would become my supervisor as Administrator of Holy Family Cemetery. Father Savoie, I thank you not only for your friendship but for the trust, freedom, and support you've given me in managing the cemetery on your behalf.

I am deeply grateful to my parents, Steven and Rebecca LeBlanc, who first instilled in me the faith that I now strive to live and serve daily in my ministry as a deacon of the Church. "May the Lord who has begun the good work in you bring it to completion."

Lastly — and most importantly — I would like to express my profound gratitude to my beloved wife, Annie. For twenty-two years, you have stood beside me with patience, love, and unwavering support. This work was often shaped in the quiet hours of the night, and without your understanding, encouragement, and sacrifice, it would not have come to fruition. I am, and will always be, eternally grateful.

TABLE OF CONTENTS

FOREWORD

Coming from a family of funeral home directors who told tales, I can appreciate how challenging but rewarding a lifetime in this industry can be. But, it shouldn't have been as difficult as it has been, where cemetery directors and others are often left guessing at applicable laws or creating forms with hopes they accomplish what they're legally intended to. This field, in Louisiana particularly, demanded a comprehensive handbook and a collection of effective and valid forms to adapt for each situation. Someone needed to step up to the plate.

Joshua LeBlanc did, thankfully. He fills this acute need with knowledge, experience, and professionalism. He has lived the life and is giving back. No one was in a better position to step up, and the professions of law, notary public, and cemetery professionals will be grateful he did. Even those who write in the general area of legal and notary forms have not filled this specific need, so before Joshua decided to share, it was good luck finding the law and the specific, valid forms. I'm proud to have co-authored with my wife, Michele, a book of 170+ Louisiana legal and notary forms, and yet our collection doesn't begin to fill this specific need. We welcome a series that does so and can be confidently applied in day-to-day practice.

Beyond providing forms in an accompanying volume, this handbook in particular methodically and comprehensively explains the laws of Louisiana and the ethical and religious obligations of those in the profession. The user will find a wealth of relevant summaries, quotations, explanations, and practical advice. It will become a consummately useful staple on the bookshelves of a wide variety of professionals in the field.

Someday, I look forward to a new edition of this work. The author can update it to fix its glaring omission: an extensive and clever workaround to Chapter 17, explaining how his cat Benedict can finally rest with Joshua. Until then, we can only hope Benedict has the endurance of a Galápagos tortoise.

Steven Alan Childress
Conrad Meyer III Professor of Law,
Tulane University Law School

INTRODUCTION

Regardless of the title you go by – Sexton, Cemetery Director, or Cemetery Authority – any person in charge of managing a cemetery in the State of Louisiana needs to have a working knowledge of Title 8 of the Louisiana Revised Statutes, known as the Louisiana Cemeteries Code. Unfortunately, many small cemeteries lack the resources to provide this knowledge or the expertise to develop proper forms that comply with Louisiana state law.

THE CULTURAL AND LEGAL LANDSCAPE OF LOUISIANA CEMETERIES

In Louisiana, the care of cemeteries is more than a matter of land use or business regulation. It is deeply bound to history, faith, and culture. From the above-ground tombs of New Orleans, shaped by geography and Catholic heritage, to the rural graveyards of Acadiana, cemeteries are sacred places where family, faith, and community meet.

All Saints' Day remains a vital tradition across the state, as families gather to whitewash tombs, lay chrysanthemums, and pay their respects to the departed. These cultural practices inform not only the appearance and ambiance of cemeteries, but also the expectations families hold for those entrusted with their care.

Overlaying this cultural reality is Louisiana's unique civil law system, inherited from France and Spain. Unlike most states, Louisiana law treats burial plots and interment rights not as fee simple real estate, but as servitudes – limited rights of use and interment, carefully defined by statute. This makes Louisiana cemetery law distinctive, requiring Cemetery Authorities to be both pastoral stewards and legal fiduciaries.

THE ROLE OF TITLE 8

The primary legal framework for cemeteries in Louisiana is Title 8 of the Louisiana Revised Statutes, which consolidates laws governing Cemetery Authorities, perpetual care funds, merchandise trusts, disinterments, rules and regulations, and succession of interment rights.

Title 8 is designed with two purposes in mind:

- Protecting families from unfair practices, lost records, or neglected grounds.
- Guiding Cemetery Authorities in fulfilling their duties as managers, trustees, and custodians of sacred ground.

This handbook closely follows Title 8, incorporating statutory text, citations, and case law that illustrate how courts and regulators have applied the law.

HOW TO USE THIS HANDBOOK

This handbook is organized to follow the life cycle of cemetery management – from creation and dedication to sales, succession, operation, and final care. The following guide will help you locate the chapters most relevant to your work or area of study.

Governance and Oversight

- If you are dealing with **cemetery governance, authority powers, or regulatory oversight**, refer to **Chapters 1–3.**
- For information on **the Louisiana Cemetery Board**, its powers, and compliance responsibilities, see **Chapter 2.**
- To learn about **rules and regulations**, including what constitutes "reasonable" limits under **La. R.S. 8:303 - 305**, see **Chapter 3.**

Cemetery Land, Dedication, and Development

- For **dedication of land for cemetery purposes** and the resulting **servitude of use**, see **Chapter 7.**
- For **removal of dedication** or **abandonment of cemetery property**, see **Chapter 8.**
- To understand **undeveloped cemetery land**, future expansion, and **development obligations after sale**, consult **Chapter 7.**

Sales, Conveyances, and Purchaser Protections

- If you are working on **sales, conveyances, or contracts**, see **Chapters 4 and 5.**
- For **consumer protection provisions, disclosure requirements,** and **right of cancellation** under **La. R.S. 8:802(F)**, see **Chapter 4.**
- For **merchandise or pre-need sales** and related **trust deposit requirements**, see **Chapter 5.**

Interment Rights, Ownership, and Succession

- For **ownership, transfer, and inheritance of interment rights**, see **Chapter 6.**
- To understand **succession without a will (intestate inheritance)** and **the personal servitude of burial use**, see **Chapter 6.**
- For **waivers, transfers, and exchanges of interment rights**, see **Chapter 6** and the *Louisiana Cemetery Forms Book.*

Burial Operations and Procedures

- For **interments, disinterments, and reinterments**, including the required authorizations, consult **Chapter 10.**
- To understand **the cemetery rules and regulations governing memorials, markers, and installations, refer to Chapter 3.**
- For **policies regarding pet interments** and freedom cemeteries have to allow or prohibit the burial of animal remains, see **Chapter 17.**

Trust Funds and Financial Management

- For **Perpetual Care Trust Funds**, including deposit requirements and annual reporting, see **Chapter 11.**
- For **Particular or Special Care funds** and their distinctions from perpetual care, also see **Chapter 11.**
- For **Merchandise and Pre-Need Trust Funds**, trustee duties, and withdrawals, see **Chapter 13.**
- Practical reporting forms for these funds appear in the *Louisiana Cemetery Forms Book.*

Abandonment and Removal of Dedication

- For **abandonment of cemetery property** and **judicial removal of dedication** under **La. R.S. 8:308–312**, see **Chapter 8.**
- For **required notices, procedural steps, and court filings**, see **Chapter 8.**
- For **best practices when reclaiming or repurposing abandoned cemetery sections**, also see **Chapter 8.**

Rules, Regulations, and Compliance

- For **creating or revising cemetery rules and regulations**, see **Chapter 3.**
- For **sample policy language** and **compliance checklists**, refer to the *Louisiana Cemetery Forms Book.*
- For **board enforcement and penalties**, see **Chapter 2.**

Consumer Relations and Liability

- For **procedures related to complaints, consumer disputes**, and **cemetery board investigations**, see **Chapter 2.**
- For **liability and negligence**, including key Louisiana cases such as *Sonnier v. Diocese of Lafayette* and *Westlawn Cemeteries v. Louisiana Cemetery Board,* see **Chapter 10.**

Cultural, Religious, and Historical Context

- For **Catholic and canonical influences** on Louisiana cemetery law, see **Chapter 14.**
- For **Louisiana's unique burial traditions** and cultural heritage, see **Chapter 14.**
- For **personal reflections** and **stories from practice**, look for the **"Grave Matters"** sidebars throughout the book.

Forms and Practical Tools

- For **sample contracts, affidavits, transfer forms, and trust clauses**, see the companion volume – the *Louisiana Cemetery Forms Book.*
- For **reporting templates, compliance checklists, and recordkeeping tools**, also see the *Forms Book.*

The Dual Role of Cemetery Authorities

As this handbook emphasizes, Cemetery Authorities serve in a dual role:

- Stewards of sacred trust, ensuring that the burial grounds remain dignified, safe, and culturally respectful.
- Legal fiduciaries, bound by Title 8 to protect funds, enforce reasonable rules, and comply with state oversight
- Navigating this dual role requires understanding both the letter of the law and the spirit of Louisiana tradition. This book seeks to provide both.

This handbook was published in November 2025

All citations from the Louisiana Revised Statutes 8 are from the 2024 edition unless otherwise noted

CHAPTER I

AN INTRODUCTION TO TITLE 8

Those in charge of cemeteries in Louisiana, Title 8 refers to as "Cemetery Authorities." In Louisiana, you are not only a steward of sacred ground – you are also responsible for operating within the framework of Louisiana Revised Statutes, Title 8 (Commonly referred to as the Louisiana Cemetery Code). This body of law governs the organization of cemeteries, the management of interment rights, and the handling of perpetual care funds.

Your role requires balancing compassion for grieving families with strict compliance with state law. This chapter outlines the key provisions of Title 8 in plain terms and explains how they apply to your day-to-day responsibilities as the Cemetery Authority.

STRUCTURE OF LOUISIANA REVISED STATUTES TITLE 8 (CEMETERIES)

Title 8 of the Louisiana Revised Statutes is devoted entirely to cemetery law. This section of the Louisiana Revised Statutes was born out of Act 417 of 1974 by the Legislature. It regulates Cemetery Authorities, interment rights, perpetual care, merchandise trust funds, mausoleum standards, handling of human remains, and related matters.

The law is divided into thirteen numbered chapters (1–13), with several sub-chapters inserted by the Legislature to address specific districts and special subject areas. This structure provides a comprehensive framework for statewide cemetery governance while allowing for local variations.

The Thirteen Chapters

Chapter 1 – Definitions **(La. R.S. 8:1)**

Provides definitions of key terms such as cemetery, interment, Cemetery Authority, trustee, and others that are used throughout Title 8.

Chapter 2 – Louisiana Cemetery Board **(La. R.S. 8:61 - 79)**

Establishes the Louisiana Cemetery Board, its membership, powers, and duties, as well as its authority over rulemaking, investigations, licensing, and enforcement actions.

Chapter 3 – Publicly Owned Cemeteries **(La. R.S. 8:101 - 114)**

Governs cemeteries owned and maintained by municipalities or parishes, including funding mechanisms, maintenance, and the establishment of required trust funds.

Chapter 4 – Cemetery Companies **(La. R.S. 8:201 - 206)**

Outlines the formation and regulation of cemetery corporations and companies, including the posting of rules and disclosure of terms in cemetery contracts.

Chapter 5 – Acquisition of Cemetery Property **(La. R.S. 8:301 - 317)**

Addresses dedication of land for cemetery use, plats and maps, removal of dedication, sales of interment spaces, abandonment procedures, and record-keeping requirements.

Chapter 6 – Cemetery Sales and Management Organizations **(La. R.S. 8:401 - 408)**

This section outlines the rules for licensing and regulating third-party cemetery sales or management entities, as well as the penalties for unauthorized practices.

Chapter 7 – Cemetery Care Fund **(La. R.S. 8:451 - 467)**

Requires cemeteries to maintain perpetual care (endowment care) trust funds, with provisions for reporting, examinations, and fiduciary management.

Chapter 8 – Merchandise Trust Fund **(La. R.S. 8:501 - 512)**

The regulation governs the preneed sales of cemetery merchandise (vaults, markers, urns, etc.) and mandates deposits into trust funds to ensure the secure delivery of goods.

Chapter 9 – Mausoleums or Similar Structures **(La. R.S. 8:601 - 606)**

Establishes construction and maintenance standards for mausoleums, columbaria, and vault structures, with enforcement against unsafe or nuisance conditions.

Chapter 10 – Human Remains **(La. R.S. 8:651 - 663)**

Sets the legal requirements for the disposition, transportation, disinterment, and reinterment of human remains, as well as provisions for liability and record-keeping.

Chapter 11 – Undeveloped Land **(La. R.S. 8:701 - 706)**

This regulation governs how Cemetery Authorities may handle, develop, and market platted cemetery land that has not yet been used for burial or interment.

Chapter 12 – Title to and Rights in Cemetery Spaces **(La. R.S. 8:801 - 814)**

Governs ownership and transfer of interment rights, including inheritance, co-ownership, transfer restrictions, and the effect of recordation.

Chapter 13 – Miscellaneous **(La. R.S. 8:901 - 908)**

Contains general provisions including burial depth requirements, prohibitions on speculative sales, public health and safety rules, and allowance for burial of pet remains in certain contexts.

Special Sub-Chapters within Title 8

In addition to the thirteen main chapters, the Legislature created several sub-chapters that supplement the general law:

Chapter 3A - 3F – Parish Cemetery Districts (St. Mary, Rapides, Grant, LaSalle, Cameron, and St. Landry Parishes).

Chapter 6A – Abandoned Cemeteries (**La. R.S. 8:411 - 418**), defining procedures for licensing and liability of abandoned cemeteries.

Chapter 10A – Louisiana Unmarked Human Burial Sites Preservation Act (**La. R.S. 8:671 - 681**), addressing discovery, permitting, and protection of unmarked burials and human skeletal remains.

Major Topics Discussed in Title 8

Interment Rights vs. Land Ownership

When you sell a space (lot, crypt, niche, etc.), you are not selling land. You are granting an interment right – the legal right to bury human remains in a specific location. Legally, you are encumbering your ownership of land with a type of *servitude* (Louisiana's language for an easement).

Cemetery Authority's Responsibilities:

- Ensure families clearly understand that a plot or niche is not "real estate."
- Maintain accurate records of who holds interment rights.
- Document how rights pass to heirs when the original purchaser dies.

Tip: Always use standardized contracts that specify "interment rights" and reference Title 8 language.

Perpetual Care Funds

Cemeteries advertising "perpetual care" must establish and maintain a trust fund. A percentage (at least 10%) of every sale must be deposited, and the income generated is used for long-term maintenance. **(La. R.S. 8:451.1c)**

Cemetery Authority's Responsibilities:

- Deposit required percentages promptly and accurately.
- Work with trustees or financial institutions to ensure funds are properly invested.
- File annual reports as required by the Louisiana Cemetery Board.
- Use income (not principal) for maintenance activities such as mowing, fence repair, and path upkeep.

> **! RISK TO AVOID:**
> Failure to maintain proper trust funds can result in regulatory penalties and loss of consumer confidence.

Burials, Disinterments, and Reinterments

Title 8 strictly regulates the removal of remains. Disinterment may only occur with a court order or the written consent of close relatives.

Cemetery Authority's Responsibilities:

- Require proper documentation before allowing any disinterment.
- Maintain written records of all removals, including documentation of family consent and court orders, to ensure accurate records and compliance with relevant laws and regulations.
- Communicate clearly with families about the legal process and expected timelines.

Example: In New Orleans, past cemetery relocations without family input led to public outcry. Title 8 ensures such actions cannot be taken unilaterally.

Oversight by the Louisiana Cemetery Board

The Louisiana Cemetery Board licenses cemeteries, enforces compliance, and investigates complaints regarding cemetery operations.

Cemetery Authority's Responsibilities:

- You must have a valid Certificate of Authority and renew it annually as required by law.
- Cooperate fully with Board inspections.
- Provide families with transparent pricing, refund policies, and disclosure of perpetual care provisions.

Tip: Keep compliance documentation organized and accessible for Board review.

Family Rights

Title 8 prioritizes families, granting them:

- Ongoing access to burial spaces.
- Succession rights to interment spaces.
- Protections against unauthorized removals.

Cemetery Authority's Responsibilities:

- Provide respectful access for visitation, including to older or less frequently visited areas of the Cemetery.

- Respect succession laws when multiple heirs claim rights to a space.
- Resolve disputes fairly, and when necessary, direct families to the Court for resolution.

Religious and Cultural Considerations

Louisiana cemeteries often reflect a blend of Catholic, Protestant, and cultural traditions, as seen in All Saints' Day celebrations. Title 8 allows religious cemeteries to operate under their own internal rules, provided they meet minimum state standards.

Cemetery Authority's Responsibilities:

- Accommodate cultural traditions when possible.
- Ensure religious rules are consistent with Title 8's requirements.
- Clearly communicate policies to families to prevent confusion and ensure understanding.

COMPLIANCE CHECKLIST

✓ Use contracts that clearly define "interment rights."
✓ Deposit perpetual care funds from each sale into the trust fund.
✓ File required reports with the Cemetery Board.
✓ Require legal documentation for disinterments.
✓ Maintain accurate and permanent burial records.
✓ Provide transparent pricing and written policies to families.
✓ Train staff on Title 8 requirements and Board regulations.

Additional Considerations Outside of Title 8

While Title 8 of the Louisiana Revised Statutes serves as the principal body of law governing cemeteries, interment rights, trust funds, and Cemetery Authorities, important cemetery-related provisions also appear in other parts of Louisiana law. These statutes either supplement Title 8 or address matters that fall outside its primary regulatory framework.

One of those areas is **La. R.S. 9:2800.24(D),** which provides that visitors have a right to visit graves, subject to reasonable restrictions.

Also to be included in these regulations is the **La. Administrative Code, Title 46, Part XIII,** which addresses Professional and Occupational Standards for the Cemetery Industry. This code is simply that — administrative codes promulgated by the Cemetery board. The Administrative code is not the same as legislative ordinances, which are statutory law. As we shall see later in this book, these codes provide rules established by the Louisiana Cemetery Board that are subject to judicial oversight. This code establishes the minimum requirements for cemetery contracts, including the duration for which deeds must be issued and the timeframe within which the Cemetery Authority must deposit perpetual care funds into the Trust. These topics will be addressed in more depth in their respective sections of this handbook.

It is also worth mentioning that the Louisiana Cemetery Board's website (lcb.la.gov) references twenty-three Attorney General Opinions regarding cemetery matters. Although Attorney General Opinions are technically advisory and do not carry the force of law, they must still be considered. It is essential to note that Attorney General opinions can be revised in light of future court decisions or newly enacted legislation.

Conclusion

Title 8 of the Louisiana Revised Statutes is not just legal text – it is the framework that protects the dignity of the deceased and the trust of the living. As a Cemetery Authority, your responsibility is twofold: to manage your cemetery with compassion and to ensure full compliance with state law. Title 8 is the Cemetery Bible!

By mastering Title 8, you safeguard your cemetery's reputation, protect families' rights, and uphold Louisiana's tradition **of treating cemeteries as sacred ground.**

CHAPTER 2

LOUISIANA CEMETERY BOARD: POWERS AND DUTIES

The Louisiana Cemetery Board (LCB) serves as the statewide regulator of cemeteries in Louisiana. Created by statute under Title 8, the Board exists to enforce the law, license Cemetery Authorities, supervise trust funds, and protect consumers.

This chapter draws from the 2024 Title 8 statutes to outline the Board's statutory powers, duties, limits, and enforcement tools, and explains how its role interacts with Cemetery Authorities.

CREATION AND STRUCTURE OF THE BOARD

Statutory Establishment

§ 8:61. Cemetery board created; appointments; terms
There is hereby created the Louisiana Cemetery Board which shall be a body corporate with power to sue and be sued, to contract and be contracted with, and to exercise all powers and duties prescribed by this Title.

Membership and Qualifications

- The Board consists of seven members appointed by the Governor, subject to confirmation by the Senate **(La. R.S. 8:62)**.

- Five members must have at least five years' experience in the Cemetery business.
    - Two members serve as public representatives, with no direct financial interest in cemeteries or funeral service businesses.

Governance

- The Board elects officers, may employ staff, and is required to meet at least twice a year **(La. R.S. 8:64 – 65)**.

Core Powers of the Board

Licensing and Certificates of Authority

- All Cemetery Authorities must submit a written application to the Board for a certificate of authority before commencing operations. **(La. R.S. 8:70)**
- Certificates must be maintained in good standing; failure to do so may result in suspension or revocation of the certificate. **(La. R.S. 8:72)**
- Operating without a certificate is a misdemeanor; each unauthorized sale or interment constitutes a separate violation. **(La. R.S. 8:74)**

Investigative and Enforcement Powers

- The Board may investigate, issue subpoenas, examine books, compel testimony, and hold hearings. **(La. R.S. 8:66.1)**
- The Board may issue cease-and-desist orders for violations, enforceable in district court. **(La. R.S. 8:66.2)**

- The Board may refuse, suspend, or revoke certificates of authority, impose fines, and seek injunctive relief against individuals or entities that violate the rules. **(La. R.S. 8:75)**
- In cases of insolvency or serious violations, the Board may seek receivership through the Attorney General to protect the public and ensure the integrity of trust funds. **(La. R.S. 8:69.2)**

Rulemaking Authority

- The Board may adopt rules "necessary to carry out the provisions of this Title," but such rules may not conflict with Title 8 or the Louisiana Constitution. **(La. R.S. 8:67)**
- Courts have confirmed that Board rules cannot overstep statutory limits, as in *Westlawn Cemeteries, LLC v. La. Cemetery Bd.*, 2022-CA-01414 (La. 2022).

Duties of the Board

Administration of Title 8

- The Board "shall enforce and administer the provisions of this Title." **(La. R.S. 8:66)**
- This includes monitoring perpetual care funds, merchandise trust funds, and consumer protections.

Oversight of Trust Funds

- Cemeteries that sell perpetual care or pre-need merchandise are required to deposit the necessary amounts into trust funds. **(La. R.S. 8:454, 601)**

- The Board requires annual reports from trustees and ensures income is properly applied to cemetery care. **(La. R.S. 8:455 - 466)**

Consumer Protection

- The Board investigates complaints from lot owners, families, and the public.
- It ensures that Cemetery Authorities disclose rules **(La. R.S. 8:454, 308)**, do not misrepresent care obligations **(La. R.S. 8:454)**, and comply with sales restrictions.

Relationship with Cemetery Authorities

Cemetery Authorities are the operators, while the Board is the regulator.

- Authorities cannot function legally without Board-issued certificates **(La. R.S. 8:70)**.
- Authorities establish trust funds, but the Board supervises compliance and reporting.
- When disputes arise, the Board acts as both watchdog and enforcement agency, with the power to fine or suspend Cemetery Authorities **(La. R.S. 8:75)**.

COMPLIANCE CHECKLIST

To fulfill its statutory mandate, the Board must:

- ✓ Appoint qualified members and hold required meetings **(La. R.S. 8:62, 65)**.
- ✓ License and renew certificates of authority **(La. R.S. 8:70)**.
- ✓ Conduct investigations into violations **(La. R.S. 8:66.1)**.
- ✓ Issue cease-and-desist orders and impose penalties where needed **(La. R.S. 8:66.2, 75)**.
- ✓ Oversee perpetual care and merchandise trust reporting **(La. R.S. 8:455 - 466)**.
- ✓ Intervene in cases of insolvency through receivership **(La. R.S. 8:69.2)**.
- ✓ Adopt rules consistent with, but not exceeding, statutory limits **(La. R.S. 8:67)**.

The Louisiana Cemetery Board exists to safeguard the public interest, enforce the provisions of Title 8, and regulate the Cemetery business. While Cemetery Authorities manage day-to-day operations, the Board ensures accountability through licensing, oversight of trust funds, and enforcement. Its powers are broad, but always bounded by statute, ensuring that both families and cemetery operators operate under explicit legal protections.

CHAPTER 3

CEMETERY AUTHORITY: POWERS AND DUTIES

Under Louisiana law, the entity responsible for owning, operating, or controlling a cemetery is known as the Cemetery Authority. The Louisiana Revised Statutes define the powers and duties of the Cemetery Authority, ensuring that cemeteries are maintained as sacred spaces, properly regulated businesses, and trustworthy institutions for families.

This chapter explores those powers and duties with reference to **La. R.S. 8:201 - 205** and related provisions, providing both direct statutory language and practical commentary.

DEFINITION OF CEMETERY AUTHORITY

The term "Cemetery Authority" is defined in Title 8 itself:

> **§ 1(8). Definitions**
> "Cemetery Authority" means any person, firm, corporation, limited liability company, trustee, partnership, association, or municipality owning, operating, controlling, or managing a cemetery or holding lands within this state for interment purposes.

This broad definition encompasses both private and public operators, including municipal, religious, and nonprofit cemeteries.

General Powers of Cemetery Authorities

Statutory Basis

In Louisiana, cemeteries are empowered to manage all aspects of interment, including selling burial spaces, establishing rules, and overseeing the maintenance and repair of property. These powers include regulating markers, monuments, plants, shrubs, and interments. They can also control visitor conduct and enforce rules for business operations, transfer of interment rights, and property protection. These powers are defined by state law, primarily in **La. R.S. 8:200 - 206.**

Specific Powers

- **Ownership and Operation** – Acquire and hold property for use as a cemetery **(La. R.S. 8:201).**
- **Sale of Interment Rights** – Sell plots, crypts, and niches, subject to the restriction that such sales convey only a right of interment, not fee title **(La. R.S. 8:304.**
- **Improvement and Maintenance** – Construct mausoleums, columbaria, chapels, and other facilities consistent with cemetery use **(La. R.S. 8:202 - 203).**
- **Adoption of Rules** – Make reasonable rules and regulations for the use and protection of the Cemetery **(La. R.S. 8:308).**
- **Trust Funds** – Establish and maintain perpetual care and merchandise trust funds when required by law **(La. R.S. 8:454; La. R.S. 8:801 - 815).**

DUTIES OF CEMETERY AUTHORITIES

With these powers come legal and fiduciary duties.

Duty of Record-Keeping

- **La. R.S. 8:501** requires the maintenance of plats and maps showing all lots, plots, crypts, and niches.
- **La. R.S. 8:502** requires a permanent register of interments, listing names of the deceased, dates, and locations.

Duty of Disclosure

Cemetery Authorities must provide families with a copy of the rules and regulations at or before the time of sale **(La. R.S. 8:308)**.

Duty of Perpetual Care (if advertised)

- If a cemetery is represented as a "perpetual care" cemetery, it must establish a perpetual care trust fund **(La. R.S. 8:454***)***.
- A portion of each sale must be deposited in trust, with the principal preserved and only income used for maintenance.

Duty to Follow Disinterment Procedures

Remains may not be moved except with the consent of the Cemetery Authority and the next of kin, or by court order **(La. R.S. 8:659)**.

Fiduciary and Managerial Obligations

- **Fiduciary Responsibility** – Cemetery Authorities act as fiduciaries when administering trust funds, bound to prudently invest and safeguard the principal for the benefit of the Cemetery community **(La. R.S. 8:454; La. R.S. 8:801 - 815)**.
- **Managerial Responsibility** – Authorities must balance compassion with compliance by providing families with access, ensuring transparent contracts, and resolving disputes fairly in accordance with Title 8.

Practical Applications

- **Sales of a Plot** – The Cemetery Authority must explain that a purchaser acquires only interment rights **(La. R.S. 8:304***)***.
- **Enforcement of Rules** – The Cemetery Authority may restrict decorations to preserve uniformity **(La. R.S. 8:308)**, but must apply the rule fairly and equitably.
- **Trust Fund Reporting** – Annual reports must be submitted to the Louisiana Cemetery Board **(La. R.S. 8:455***)***.
- **Family Dispute** – If heirs disagree on succession to a plot, the Cemetery Authority may rely on an affidavit of heirship **(La. R.S. 8:802), but** should not inter a body until the disputes are resolved.

COMPLIANCE CHECKLIST

- ✓ Maintain plats, maps, and burial registers **(La. R.S. 8:501 - 502)**.
- ✓ Provide written rules and contracts **(La. R.S. 8:308)**.
- ✓ Deposit perpetual care and merchandise funds as required **(La. R.S. 8:454; La. R.S. 8:801 - 815)**.
- ✓ Obtain proper consent before disinterments **(La. R.S. 8:659)**.
- ✓ Apply rules consistently and reasonably **(La. R.S. 8:308)**.

Conclusion

The powers and duties of Cemetery Authorities in Louisiana strike a balance: they have broad authority to own and operate cemeteries, but equally weighty responsibilities to maintain records, safeguard funds, and respect the statutory rights of families, as outlined in Title 8. With diligence and transparency, Cemetery Authorities uphold both the law and the sacred trust of caring for the dead.

RIP

GRAVE MATTERS
Personal Reflections of a Cemetery Director

WITH GREAT POWER COMES GREAT RESPONSIBILITY

As a Deacon, one of the areas I have spent a fair amount of time in is pastoral ministry, which primarily focuses on the individual and what is in their best interest. As the **Director of a Cemetery**, I have had to adapt to the broader responsibility of ensuring the **common good** for all those buried at my cemetery.

One of the most challenging roles I have been assigned is **enforcing the cemetery's rules and regulations**, particularly in cases of **non-compliance.** As a **Cemetery Director**, my job is to consider the **common good** and to establish **standards** that make the cemetery **appealing to all**. In a real way, there is a **categorical imperative** here – rules must be established while considering the following: *"If everyone is allowed to do this, is it good for the cemetery?"*

When I first started in my role, I faced the challenge not of creating new rules but of **enforcing rules that had long existed but had not been applied.** As you can imagine, some were **not happy.** Still, the number of individuals who **thanked me for the uniformity** and for the **overall beauty** that this enforcement has accomplished has far outweighed the naysayers.

I offer this as a reminder that being the **"bad guy"** at times requires **fortitude and courage.** Still, in the end, it pays off when visitors notice that the **overall appearance** of your cemetery has improved, as well as with **new customers** who want to purchase spaces in your cemetery because of these qualities.

The work of a **Cemetery Director** is often difficult and thankless, but if we remain true to the work we do—keeping in mind that we are **entrusted to care for all those buried in our midst**—then the **reward** we seek is not a *pat on the back*, but is instead found in the **appearance, orderliness**, and **reverence** of the sacred grounds we manage.

CHAPTER 4

PERSONAL SERVITUDE OF A RIGHT OF USE IN LOUISIANA

In Louisiana, the sale or grant of a cemetery lot does not transfer ownership of the underlying land. Instead, the purchaser receives a personal servitude, which is a right of use and possession. This is a legally recognized real right of use, limited to the specific purpose of interring human remains. The cemetery corporation or religious authority retains ownership of the land itself. This is an important distinction, especially as it relates to conveyances such as sales contracts or transfers of burial rights.

Too often, notaries and attorneys send Cemetery Authority paperwork, such as affidavits or transfers to third parties, describing these burial rights as real, immovable property. As a Cemetery Authority, it is your prerogative to make sure that the paperwork that you approve for transfer is both accurate in its language and in its description of burial rights.

CHARACTER

The right of use is classified under Louisiana Civil Law as a personal servitude (see Articles 534 through 645 of the Civil Code). It grants the holder the authority to use a designated portion of cemetery property exclusively for the interment of human remains. The right may not be expanded to any other use, nor may it be exercised in a manner contrary to the Cemetery's rules and regulations.

PERPETUAL AND HERITABLE NATURE

Perpetual: The personal servitude of a right of burial is generally perpetual in character. Once established, it remains attached to the designated space and does not expire with time (except for burials in the City of New Orleans – see **La. R.S. 8:308(B)**).

Heritable: The right is inheritable under the Louisiana succession law. Upon the holder's death, the heirs succeed to the right, ensuring the continuity of family burial privileges. Title 8 provides two methods by which the owner can designate a cemetery space as inalienable — that is, the burial rights cannot be transferred, sold, or taken away. This is essentially a way for the owner of multiple spaces to designate who can be buried in those spaces. The two methods that **La. R.S. 8:805** denote:

- In a form approved by the Cemetery Authority
- In the last will and testament of the owner to the Cemetery in perpetual trust.

§ 805. When right of interment or cemetery space is inalienable
Subject to the approval of the Cemetery Authority, any cemetery space in any cemetery may be conveyed by the owner or owners, by proper instrument in a form approved by the Cemetery Authority, or such conveyance may be so provided in the last will and testament of the owner to the Cemetery Authority in perpetual trust for its preservation as a place of interment and shall thereafter remain forever inalienable by act of the parties. The right to use the Cemetery space as a place of interment of the dead of the family of the owner and his descendants shall descend from generation to generation, unless the act of conveyance in trust provides that interments in the space shall be confined to the remains of specified persons, in which case the space shall be forever preserved for the remains of the persons so specified and shall never be used for any other purpose.

While the Cemetery can prepare its own form, indicating the space information and the person who is permitted to be buried in that space, and such a designation would be sufficient, it is always a good idea to have such a declaration made in the form of a notarial declaration.

As indicated in Title 8, such a trust can be created *mortis causa*, that is, in what is called a testamentary trust in the Last Will and Testament. In this form, the testator (the owner) specifies the burial spaces and who is permitted to be buried in them, with the Cemetery listed as the trustee. The owner can also transfer ownership of spaces to individuals, rather than simply designating who is to be buried in those spaces. One way this is accomplished is through an Act of Donation.

The former option provides the Cemetery with greater reliability, as it utilizes the Cemetery's form; the Cemetery Authority can be certain that burial spaces are accurately described. When the designation occurs in a will, the Cemetery Authority may not even be aware of this act. If the burial spaces described are inaccurate, it would be difficult to rectify the situation, as the deceased owner cannot provide clarification or correction.

However, burial privileges are limited to available empty burial spaces. **La. R.S. 8:811** notes that there is no right to burial in a space which already contains an interment:

> **§ 811. Limitations on vested rights**
> No vested right of interment gives to any person the right to have his remains interred in any interment space in which the remains of any deceased person having a prior vested right of interment have been interred, nor does it give any person the right to have the remains of more than one deceased person interred in a single interment space in violation of the rules and regulations of the Cemetery Authority of the Cemetery in which the interment space is located.

Transferable: While the rights may sometimes be transferred, such transfers are subject to the Cemetery's governing policies, as outlined in **La. R.S. 8:802** requires written approval and recordation by the Cemetery Authority.

> **§ 802(A). Transfer of ownership rights**
> In order to insure that at all times the Cemetery Authority will have complete and accurate records, the sale or transfer of any right of interment or cemetery space, shall not be binding upon a Cemetery Authority until approved in writing by a duly authorized officer, agent or employee of the Cemetery Authority and duly recorded in the official records of the Cemetery.

Distinction from Land Ownership

Purchasers of cemetery plots often believe they are acquiring ownership of land. In fact, they acquire only the servitude of a right to burial. The land itself remains the property of the Cemetery. The purchaser and heirs, however, hold an enforceable legal right to use the designated space for interment, protected under Louisiana law.

Protection of the Servitude

Louisiana law provides strict safeguards once human remains have been interred:

- Graves may not be disturbed except through formal disinterment and reinterment procedures authorized by law.
- The Cemetery Authority must honor the perpetual burial right, subject to reasonable regulation of maintenance and operation.
- Families also retain the right of visitation and upkeep, consistent with cemetery policies.

The right of visitation noted above is codified in **La. R.S. 9**, which states:

La. R.S. 9:2800.24(D)
Limitation of liability for granting voluntary right of passage to enclosed Cemetery
A voluntary right of passage otherwise available by law to visitors and descendants cannot be unreasonably withheld by the owner, but may be limited to reasonable times and durations and may follow a path designated by the owner

Cemetery Authority's Responsibilities

Cemetery Authorities must ensure that families understand the nature of their rights at the time of purchase. Written instruments should clarify:

- The family acquires a personal servitude – not ownership of land but a right to burial.
- That the right is heritable and continues through succession.
- The right is subject to cemetery rules and state law, including restrictions on transfer and use.

Cemetery Authorities should also safeguard the records of interments and plot rights, as these records establish the legal basis for the burial servitude across generations.

COMPLIANCE CHECKLIST

- ✓ Confirm that purchasers acquire a **personal servitude of a right of use**, not ownership of land **(La. Civ. Code arts. 534 - 645)**.
- ✓ Use only **Cemetery Authority-approved forms** for all sales or transfers, with **written approval and recordation** in official records **(La. R.S. 8:802(A))**.
- ✓ Ensure all documents and marketing materials **avoid describing burial rights as real or immovable property.**
- ✓ Clearly state that the right is **perpetual and heritable**, except where otherwise limited **(La. R.S. 8:308(B))**.
- ✓ When a space is made **inalienable**, confirm that it is established by a Cemetery-Approved form or testamentary trust **(La. R.S. 8:805)**.
- ✓ Verify **no interment occurs in occupied spaces** and that all burials follow Cemetery rules **(La. R.S. 8:811)**.
- ✓ Maintain **permanent records** of purchasers, heirs, transfers, and designations; back up both paper and digital files.
- ✓ Provide each purchaser with a **written disclosure** explaining that the Cemetery retains land ownership.
- ✓ Allow **reasonable visitation and access for upkeep consistent with Louisiana law. R.S. 9:2800.24(D)** and Cemetery policy.
- ✓ Conduct **annual internal audits** to verify compliance with Title 8, record accuracy, and policy enforcement.

Conclusion

The personal servitude of a right of use lies at the very heart of Louisiana cemetery law. It defines the nature of the relationship between the Cemetery Authority and the families it serves, ensuring that sacred grounds remain under unified stewardship while granting perpetual, heritable rights of burial to individuals and their heirs. By understanding that a cemetery space conveys not ownership of land but a distinct legal right of interment, Cemetery Authorities can properly manage transfers, recordkeeping, and family expectations within the bounds of law.

Accurate documentation, consistent terminology, and careful record preservation are essential to maintaining compliance with Title 8 and the Civil Code. When Cemetery Authorities uphold these principles, they protect the dignity of the deceased, the trust of the living, and the integrity of the cemetery's perpetual mission. Through sound administration and clear communication, the personal servitude of burial becomes more than a legal concept – it remains a lasting covenant between generations and the sacred ground they share.

GRAVE MATTERS
Personal Reflections of a Cemetery Director

SELLING WHAT CANNOT BE OWNED

One of the most common misconceptions I encounter as a Cemetery Director is the belief that when someone buys a burial space, they are **purchasing land.** In truth, they are acquiring a **right of use** – a sacred permission, not ownership. The land itself remains **dedicated ground**, set apart forever for the **burial of the dead** and subject to the perpetual care and protection of the cemetery authority, who has the right and responsibility to manage and direct its property.

This distinction between **ownership** and **right of use** is more than a technicality; it reflects a **theological truth** about the dignity of the human person and the sanctity of the ground in which we lay them to rest. The law recognizes that cemetery land cannot be treated like ordinary real estate – it is **sacred trust property**, permanently restricted to the purpose of interment.

For this reason, when a person **sells or transfers** a right of use, they are not selling soil or structure but **the privilege to rest within it** – a right that carries both **responsibility and reverence.** It is why every transfer must be handled carefully, appropriately documented, and always in keeping with the cemetery's rules and the Church's moral understanding of **sacred space.**

It may seem like paperwork and policy, but beneath it lies something deeper: the call to **steward what is holy.** We are not merchants of land; we are **guardians of the resting place.** To sell what cannot truly be owned is to remind ourselves that even in death, **we belong not to the earth, but to God.**

CHAPTER 5

UNDEVELOPED CEMETERY LAND

Cemetery Authorities in Louisiana often acquire land in anticipation of future growth. While it is permissible to hold undeveloped land for eventual use as a cemetery, the development of that land must comply with statutory requirements to ensure public trust, protect purchasers, and uphold the dignity of burial grounds.

DEDICATION OF CEMETERY LAND

Once land is formally dedicated for cemetery purposes under **La. R.S. 8:304,** it becomes subject to a servitude of use. This means the land cannot be used for any purpose other than interment, unless and until a court authorizes the removal of dedication pursuant to **La. R.S. 8:308 - 312.**

Cemetery Authorities may hold land for future expansion, but dedication and subsequent sales carry with them legal obligations to develop that land into functional burial property.

DEVELOPMENT REQUIREMENTS AFTER SALE

When interment spaces are sold in an undeveloped section, Louisiana law requires the Cemetery Authority to develop the property within specific timelines:

- **Undeveloped Land**: Development must begin within 24 months of the first sale and be completed within 48 months. **(La. R.S. 8:706)**
- **Mausoleums and Columbaria:** Construction must begin within 48 months of the first sale in a section, and that section must be completed within 5 years. **(La. R.S. 8:606)**

Failure to meet these deadlines may result in enforcement actions, refunds, or penalties.

Minimum Standards for Burial Depth

Louisiana also regulates the physical standards for in-ground burials. **La. R.S. 8:902** provides for the minimum depth requirements of graves:

§ 902. Underground burials; depth
Any cemetery sexton or other person digging graves for underground interments shall dig sufficiently deep to allow for at least two feet of soil to cover the entire area of the casket, unless the interment is in a burial vault, coping, or lawn crypt.

Where water tables or soil conditions make this impracticable, above-ground burial structures (such as vaults or tombs) are permissible and widely used, especially in coastal and flood-prone areas, like New Orleans.

Cemetery Authorities are responsible for ensuring compliance with these depth requirements.

Platting and Record-Keeping

Before undeveloped land can be sold as interment space, the Cemetery Authority must comply with platting and record-keeping requirements:

- Prepare plats and maps showing the layout of sections, lots, and interment spaces. **(La. R.S. 8:305 - 305.1)**
- Maintain a permanent register of interments, listing the deceased's name, burial date, and location. **(La. R.S. 8:662)**

These records provide transparency and help resolve disputes regarding interment rights.

Fiduciary Obligations

Funds received from the sale of spaces in undeveloped land must be used in compliance with trust fund statutes:

- **Perpetual Care Trust Fund (La. R.S. 8:454***)* – If the Cemetery is advertised as "perpetual care," a portion of each sale must be deposited into this trust.
- **Preneed and Merchandise Trusts (La. R.S. 8:801 - 815)** – If sales include preneed merchandise or services, deposits into a merchandise trust are required.

Cemetery Authorities are fiduciaries of these funds and must account for them in their annual reports to the Louisiana Cemetery Board **(La. R.S. 8:455)**.

Practical Considerations

- **Phased Development** – Many cemeteries develop land in stages, ensuring demand matches investment.
- **Environmental Challenges** – Soil conditions, flood zones, and water tables may affect whether land is suitable for below-ground interments.
- **Transparency** – Families must be informed of development timelines, particularly for mausoleums and columbaria.

COMPLIANCE CHECKLIST

- ✓ Verify that all property dedicated for cemetery purposes complies with La. R.S. 8:304, and that once dedicated, the land is used exclusively for interment until a court formally removes the dedication (**La. R.S. 8:308 – 312**).
- ✓ Before selling any space in an undeveloped section, prepare and file plats and maps that show the layout of sections, lots, and spaces in accordance with **La. R.S. 8:305 – 305.1**.
- ✓ Ensure that a permanent register of interments is maintained listing each decedent's name, date of burial, and location (**La. R.S. 8:662**).
- ✓ Begin development of undeveloped land within 24 months of the first sale and complete development within 48 months, as required by **La. R.S. 8:706**.
- ✓ For mausoleum or columbarium sections, begin construction within 48 months of the first sale and complete the project within five years (**La. R.S. 8:606**).
- ✓ Verify that all graves are dug to the statutory depth — at least two feet of soil above the casket, unless an approved vault, coping, or lawn crypt is used (**La. R.S. 8:902**).
- ✓ Conduct soil and water-table assessments to confirm that below-ground interment is feasible; use above-ground structures where necessary due to environmental conditions.
- ✓ Deposit the proper percentage of each sale into the Perpetual Care Trust Fund when the cemetery is designated as perpetual-care (**La. R.S. 8:454 – 455**).
- ✓ Deposit required funds for any preneed or merchandise sales into a merchandise trust in compliance with **La. R.S. 8:801 – 815**, and report annually to the Louisiana Cemetery Board.
- ✓ Provide written disclosure to purchasers of development timelines, phased construction plans, and any conditions affecting when interment can occur.

Conclusion

Undeveloped land is both an opportunity and a responsibility for Cemetery Authorities. Once interment spaces are sold, Louisiana law imposes strict requirements: platting before sale, construction deadlines, burial depth standards, and trust fund obligations. By diligently following Title 8, Cemetery Authorities protect consumer trust and ensure cemeteries remain sacred, orderly, and financially sustainable.

GRAVE MATTERS

Personal Reflections of a Cemetery Director

THE WRITING ON THE WALL

One of the phrases I've heard the most as a Cemetery Director is, *"But I own that land!"* The biggest **misnomer** that exists in cemeteries is the belief that those purchasing **burial rights** truly understand what they are purchasing. It is this **misunderstanding** that often leads to **rule violations** and **hurt feelings** among those who purchase burial rights in a cemetery.

The importance of **written contracts**—in fact, **putting everything in writing**—cannot be understated. In times of **grief**, families are often not thinking clearly, precisely because they are focused on navigating that complex process. For this reason, in addition to **explaining everything verbally**, I ensure that I **document everything** and have families **sign off** on the process. This provides **transparency**, helps prevent **misunderstandings**, and gives the **Cemetery Authority** a solid foundation to stand on when issues arise later.

A good example is to **never rely on obituaries** for dates on monuments. I once came across an obituary that listed **two different dates of birth**—neither of which was correct. Before ordering any plaques or memorials, I always generate an **approval rendering** with the proposed dates and have the **family member sign off** on it. This small step has helped tremendously in avoiding **errors** and in identifying **where a mistake originated** when one occurred.

For this reason, I cannot say it enough – **PUT EVERYTHING IN WRITING!** Families appreciate **clarity and accountability**, and the cemetery gains **peace of mind** knowing it did everything possible to **communicate clearly**, prevent confusion, and **protect the trust** placed in its care.

CHAPTER 6

SALES AND OTHER CONVEYANCES BY THE CEMETERY AUTHORITY

Cemetery sales are unlike ordinary real estate transactions. In Louisiana, when a family purchases a burial space, they are not acquiring land but rather a **right of interment** – a legal right to use a designated burial space. Title 8 of the Louisiana Revised Statutes sets the framework for these sales, ensuring that families understand what they are buying and that cemeteries maintain proper records and practices.

As a Cemetery Authority, you are responsible for managing these transactions with both **legal precision** and **pastoral sensitivity**. This chapter explains how sales and conveyances operate under Louisiana law and provides guidance on best practices for these transactions.

Cemetery Authorities can think of the Cemetery office as analogous to a parish Clerk of Court, just as a clerk of Court contains all the records of the parish regarding land records and conveyances. Hence, the Cemetery office is responsible for recording and maintaining accurate records of all conveyances of burial rights in the Cemetery. It is for this reason that no conveyance of a cemetery transaction is recorded with a clerk of Court – they are recorded **only** with the Cemetery itself.

The Nature of the Transaction: Interment Rights vs. Real Property

- A sale conveys a **right of interment**, not ownership of the land. This right of interment is a servitude that encumbers the Cemetery's property, granting to the owner the right to be buried in that space.
- Families cannot resell the property as real estate; they can only transfer or assign the burial right to the extent it is allowed by the Cemetery's rules and regulations or as designated by the original owner. Some cemeteries restrict individuals' right to resell their burial rights, requiring that any rights be sold back to the Cemetery, while others allow third-party transactions. In any case, **La. R.S. 8:802 requires the permission of the Cemetery Authority for a conveyance of burial rights to another party.**
- This distinction protects cemeteries from subdivision or treatment as commercial real estate.

Cemetery Authority's Role:

Always explain this distinction clearly in contracts and during meetings with families.

Sales Procedures

Cemetery transactions in Louisiana require written contracts, which are governed by **Title 46, XIII - 909** of the Administrative Code. This article in the administrative code establishes the minimum requirements for cemetery contracts:

La. Admin. Code tit. 46, XIII – 909
A. All contracts for cemetery spaces, interment rights, or cemetery related merchandise and services shall be in writing and written in clear and understandable language. All such contracts shall be sequentially numbered and entered into a sales journal numerically.

B. All contracts under Subsection 909. A shall include the following mandatory information:
1. date of the contract;
2. name of the seller and purchaser;
3. statement that the Cemetery is perpetual care, if applicable;
4. the location of the interment space;
5. an itemization of the prices charged, including any applied discounts, for each item provided as part of the contract;
6. the terms under which each contract is to be paid; and
7. the clear terms for cancellation of the agreement and the damages for cancellation, if any.

C. All contracts for cemetery spaces or interment rights shall also include:
1. the cost of the Cemetery space or interment right(s);
2. the type of interment to be provided and the number of interments allowed. Nothing in this Section shall be interpreted to limit the ability of a Cemetery Authority to sell or allow multiple interments, as permitted by the Cemetery Authority's rules;
3. the amount or percentage to be placed in the Cemetery's perpetual or endowed care trust; and
4. a statement regarding whether the payment for the Cemetery space(s) or interment right(s) includes or does not include the cost of opening and closing of the Cemetery space.

D. All contracts for Cemetery related merchandise and services shall also include:
1. the price of each item of merchandise or service contracted for;
2. if the merchandise will not be delivered or stored pursuant to R.S. 8:502.1, then the agreement shall state the amount or percentage to be placed in the Cemetery's merchandise trust fund;
3. a description of each item of merchandise or service with sufficient information to describe the merchandise or service, including the size, design, and materials used in construction or manufacture.

Sales/Conveyances of Cemetery burial rights, although they are not sales of real property, do involve an encumbrance of real property. In Louisiana, transactions involving real property typically need to be recorded with the clerk of Court and must also be an Authentic Act.

An Authentic Act is a term in the state of Louisiana for an agreement signed by the relevant parties and two witnesses before a notary public, in the case of cemetery conveyances, **La. R.S. 8:812 merely requires that the act of conveyance be done on a form "prescribed by the Cemetery Authority" and, once signed by the purchaser and the Cemetery Authority, that any such conveyance is an Authentic Act as though it was passed before a notary public and two witnesses.**

IMPORTANT:

This is a notable *exception* under the law. This author knows of no other instance in which only the signatures of the purchaser and the seller qualify as an Authentic Act.

For practical purposes, this means that only the purchaser and the seller need to sign a cemetery sales agreement, and that agreement is self-proving in a court of law. Such an act does not need to be filed in any public office (such as the clerk of Court).

§ 812. Conveyance of cemetery spaces; formality and recordation

Cemetery Authorities that own land destined as places for the interment of human remains may convey portions thereof, or cemetery spaces located therein, for interments. The acts of conveyance shall be passed under the form prescribed by the Cemetery Authority, and any acts so made shall be equally authentic and impart full proof as if passed before a notary and two witnesses. It shall not be necessary to record such instruments in any public office.

This statute **creates an exception** to the authentic-form rule – **but only for transfers and sales made under Title 8**, i.e., transactions between a cemetery authority and a purchaser.

APPLICATION OF LA. R.S. 8:812 TO AFFIDAVITS AND CEMETERY INSTRUMENTS

Instrument Type	Is Authentic Form Required by La. R.S. 8:812?	Notes / Reasoning
Interment Right Sale or Transfer	❌ Not required between parties	Must be **in writing**; only **acknowledgment or Authentic Form** needed if it will be **recorded** in parish conveyance records, which is not required.
Assignment of Interment Rights	❌ Not required between parties	Authentic Form recommended for evidentiary value or filing in parish conveyance records, which is not required.
Waiver of Interment Rights	✅ Yes	**Authentic Form** is required because individuals do not normally give up the rights to things. **La. C.C art. 1541.**
Dation en Paiement of Burial Space	✅ Yes	This is a *civil code dation* (**La. C.C. art. 2655**), not a mere Title 8 sale; must be authentic.
Affidavit of Heirship or Ownership for Burial Space	⚠️ Optional	May be by acknowledgment; authentic form is required only if it is to be **recorded** for notice.

Instrument Type	Is Authentic Form Required by La. R.S. 8:812?	Notes / Reasoning
Declaration or Trust Affecting Burial Space	⚠️ Usually advisable	Title 8 doesn't require authentic form, but **La. R.S. 9:1752** (Trust Code) allows either **authentic or acknowledged** form.
Servitude or Easement for Cemetery Access	✅ Yes	This is a *real servitude* under the Civil Code – must be an Authentic Act.
Designation of Burial Rights within a Family	⚠️ Not required by statute	For long-term enforceability, an authentic form is recommended.

Acts of Donation and the Required Form

Scenario	Governing Law	Form Required	Reasoning
Donation by Cemetery Authority to Purchaser (a Title 8 "conveyance")	**La. R.S. 8:812**	Writing suffices; Authentic Act is not required unless recorded	Treated as a sale or conveyance under Title 8
Donation by Private Owner of Interment Right to Another Person (family or third party)	**La. C.C. art. 1536**	**Authentic Act required**	Donations *inter vivos* of rights require an Authentic act when Cemetery is not a party.

Practical Summary

Purpose	Authentic Form Required	Citation
Cemetery ↔ Purchaser	❌ No	Covered by **La, R.S. 8:812(A)**; written signature sufficient.
Private ↔ Private Transfer	❌ No	**La. C.C. art. 1839** allows transactions to be passed by Authentic Act or under private signature.
Donation / Dation / Partition	✅ Yes	Governed by **La. C.C. arts. 1536, 2655, 807.**

Key Points:

La. R.S. 8:812 creates a *limited exception* to Louisiana's general authentic-act rule: a cemetery deed, sale, or transfer is valid between the cemetery authority and the purchaser even without authentic form, but an authentic or acknowledged form is still **required for recordation** and **third-party protection.**

Transparency in Pricing

Cemeteries should disclose **all fees** (interment charges, marker installation, maintenance assessments, etc.) Although a general price list is not required for funeral homes, it is good practice to provide families with one at the time of purchase, and to indicate whether prices are subject to change.

Families **must** receive an itemized contract and a copy of the Cemetery **rules. La. R.S. 8:205** provides guidance here on the minimum requirements for the availability of Cemetery Rules:

> **§ 205. Rules and regulations; posting**
> The rules and regulations made pursuant to R.S. 8:204 shall be plainly printed or typewritten and maintained subject to inspection in the office of the Cemetery Authority.

ISSUANCE OF INTERMENT RIGHTS TITLE/DEED

Please note that the Cemetery Authority **must** issue a Title/Deed for a cemetery space within 30 days after payment in full. The statute stating this requirement reads as follows:

> **La. Admin. Code tit. 46, XIII – 2303(A):**
> **Issuance of Documents Reflecting Title and Rights in Cemetery Spaces**
> The Cemetery shall issue a title or certificate of interment right to the purchaser or transferee within 30 days of payment in full of the contract or transfer, if made without charge.

OWNER OF BURIAL RIGHTS

An important distinction to note is that the person who purchases the burial rights is not always the owner of said rights. It is important to note that **La. R.S. 8:205** provides clarity on this fact:

§ 801. Recognized owner of title
The person or persons or entity in whose names the official title to a cemetery space appears in the official records of a Cemetery Authority shall be treated as the owner of said space by the Cemetery Authority.

As a matter of procedure, a Cemetery Authority should never issue a Deed for a cemetery space to a decedent, as a deceased person cannot be placed in ownership of anything, including burial rights. Additionally, you may encounter well-meaning individuals who wish to purchase a burial space and have it placed in the name of their child, brother, uncle, or other loved one. Even though a purchaser is not purchasing real property, they are buying a *servitude* — an encumbrance on *real property*. As a general rule, Cemetery Authorities should never allow someone to purchase burial rights and put them in someone else's name without the purchaser's express written consent.

A better practice would be to register the burial space in the name of the person purchasing it and then provide a declaration, preferably notarized, stating who is permitted to be buried in those spaces. It is also possible to have a notary later prepare an Act of Donation. This method is preferable because an Act of Donation requires the recipient to accept the donation for it to be valid. Therefore, there is no transfer of interment rights in a burial space without the knowledge of the person in whose name it is being transferred.

In any case, the person to whom the deed itself is issued is to be considered the owner of the burial space, which is why it is essential to make this distinction clear on the contract as well. This grants the owner the right to dispose of the interment rights as they see fit, in accordance with cemetery rules and regulations.

OTHER CONVEYANCES AND TRANSFERS

Inheritance: Because burial spaces in Louisiana are considered community property if purchased while married, the living spouse of the deceased owner is regarded as a co-owner of the burial space. If there is an unoccupied space for the burial of that spouse, they have a vested right to interment in that space **(La. R.S. 8:806)**. If purchased by the owner and the owner was not married at the time, it would most likely be considered separate property, even if the owner later marries.

Interment rights pass by **succession** upon the owner's death. This is probably one of the most challenging situations Cemetery Authorities will encounter, as the inheritance of burial spaces can cause confusion in locating heirs and also be a source of contention among them. These situations must be handled with care and accuracy. If the Cemetery does not exercise due diligence, it can cause undue hardship and anguish to families and lead to legal issues, especially when individuals are buried in spaces they may not have the right to occupy. **La. R.S. 8:803** provides the Cemetery Authority with guidance:

§ 803. Descent of title to cemetery space
Except as otherwise provided in this Chapter, every right of interment and Cemetery space shall be subject to the laws of this state pertaining to community property, inheritance, including but not limited to the laws of intestacy, donations *inter vivos* and *mortis causa*, and successions. Heirs must provide proof of succession or an affidavit of heirship to exercise rights.

In Louisiana, how the burial spaces descend will depend on whether the owner had died testate (with a will) or intestate (without a will). In the case of a will, the will controls who has the right to these burial spaces. In cases where there is no will, then the laws of inheritance will prevail. See chart below (extrapolated from **La. Civil Code 880 et seq.)**

ORDER OF INHERITANCE WITH NO WILL (INTESTATE)

Community Property	Separate Property
Spouse (or other co-owners) has a vested right to buria in any unused space (La. R.S. 8.805), then;	To children (or their descendants, if children are deceased). If no children, then ↓
To children (or their descendents, if the children are deceased). If no children, then; ↓	To brothers and sisters (or if any of them are deceased, their descendants). If no brothers or sisters (or their descendants) are alive, then
Cemetery space is treated as separate property and passes as noted in the "Separate Property" column.	To spouse. If there is no spouse, then ↓ To grandparents or other ascendants. If nobody exists in this group, then To nearest relative.

This chart is provided as a general guideline only. Because every situation is unique, it is always advisable to consult an attorney for specific or complex matters.

If the owner acquired the space while married, the spouse has a vested interest in any unused burial spaces after the owner's burial, because burial spaces are subject to the laws of community property **(La. R.S. 8:803)**. This right is a usufruct-like right in the sense that usufructs are granted to the surviving spouse until they die or some other triggering life event. However, in this case, the spouse's right to be buried in such a space occurs at death, granting them the right to be buried there in perpetuity.

Waiver of Interment Rights

La. R.S. 8:809 provides that an heir, who has a right to interment in a space, may waive that right **in favor of another relative or spouse of the deceased record owner:**

> **§ 809. Waiver of right of interment**
> Any surviving spouse, parent, child, or heir having a right of interment in an interment space may waive such right in favor of any other relative or spouse of a relative of the deceased record owner. Upon such waiver, the remains of the person in whose favor the waiver is made may be interred in the interment space.

When rights to interment terminate

Burial rights can be terminated voluntarily if waived by the party who holds such an interment right, or if that person is interred elsewhere. This is an essential point for a Cemetery Authority because if a person is buried in another cemetery, they no longer have a vested right of interment in their original cemetery space. It is important to note that this statute concerns the rights of those who are heirs as mentioned in the preceding two paragraphs **(La. R.S. 8:809 – 810).** In other words, a family member who would typically be an heir to a burial space has their rights to burial in that space terminated if they are buried elsewhere. This provision does not apply to original owners, as the burial rights purchased are subject to the laws of inheritance, as noted in **La. R.S. 8:803.**

> **§ 810. Termination of vested right by waiver**
> A vested right of interment may be waived and is terminated upon the interment elsewhere of the remains of the person in whom vested.

Resale or Assignment: Families may sell or assign unused interment rights, provided they obtain permission from the Cemetery Authority and comply with its rules and regulations. They cannot resell or assign the rights to another person if doing so would be in direct conflict with the owner having filed a declaration of inalienability (**La. R.S. 8:805**).

Cemetery Authorities must update cemetery records to reflect new right-holders.

Cemeteries may impose reasonable restrictions, such as requiring transfers to proceed through the Cemetery office as well as payment of fees to the Cemetery's Perpetual Care fund by the new right holders (**La. Attorney General Opinion 89 – 0565**).

Tip: Require all transfers to be documented with proper instruments and recorded in the Cemetery records.

Protest by Owner: The owner of a burial space can protest the burial of someone else in their burial space, according to **La. R.S. 8:802(E)**. It does not appear that this objection is limited to the surviving heirs, but also by the declaration of the owner themselves:

§802. Transfer of ownership rights
E. Whenever a cemetery authority makes an interment on the authority of a person who presents the official title to the cemetery space in which the interment is to be made, the right of the cemetery authority to make the interment shall be conclusively presumed, but it shall have the right to refuse to permit an interment if it receives a written protest from any person who, in the sole judgment of an officer of the cemetery authority, has a reasonable basis for objecting.

The right to file a protest under this statute would also logically extend to the record owner of a cemetery space. An owner who wishes to restrict or prohibit a specific individual from being interred in the space they own may submit a written letter of protest to the cemetery authority. Once received, this letter serves as a formal notice of objection, and the cemetery authority may, under the statute, refuse to permit the interment of the person identified in the protest. This filing effectively places the matter in suspension until the protest is withdrawn, resolved between the parties, or adjudicated by a court of competent jurisdiction.

It is essential to acknowledge that the statute does not require the cemetery to deny burial in every instance of protest; instead, it grants the cemetery discretion to do so if, in its sole judgment, the written objection is based on reasonable grounds. This ensures that the Cemetery Authority may exercise prudence in balancing the rights of the owner, the wishes of the family, and the integrity of its records, without being compelled to act on frivolous or malicious objections.

In any situation where there is uncertainty, a dispute, or competing claims to burial rights, the cemetery should consult with qualified legal counsel before taking any action. If the matter cannot be amicably resolved, the safest and most lawful course is to petition the appropriate district court for a declaratory judgment or order determining who holds the valid right of interment. Such a judicial determination provides the Cemetery Authority with legal protection and ensures that all parties' rights are properly respected under Louisiana law.

Record-Keeping Requirements

Accurate records are the backbone of cemetery operations. Title 8 requires cemeteries to keep:

- A master plat of the Cemetery showing spaces sold and unsold.
- Individual ownership records for each interment right.
- Copies of contracts, titles/deeds, transfers, and assignments.
- Burial registers documenting interments.

Cemetery Authority's Role:

- Use both paper and digital records for redundancy.
- Back up digital systems regularly.
- Make records available for inspection by the Louisiana Cemetery Board.

Special Considerations

Perpetual Care Cemeteries

For cemeteries advertising perpetual care:

- A percentage of each sale (at least 10%) must be deposited into the Perpetual Care Trust Fund. **(La. R.S. 8:454.1(C))**
- Sales staff should clearly explain how these funds are utilized and why they are important.
- Deposit Perpetual Care funds into trust accounts within 30 days following the month in which they are collected per **La. Admin. Code tit. 46, XIII - 1501.**

Pre-need Sales

- Families may purchase spaces in advance.
- Funds from pre-need sales must be handled carefully, with deposits into trust accounts as required. This provision does not apply to family burial grounds, or religious, fraternal, municipal, state, or federal cemeteries **(La. R.S. 8:510)**.
- Cemetery Authorities should ensure compliance with pre-need statutes and regulations.

Religious or Municipal Cemeteries

- Religious cemeteries may follow internal rules, but conveyances must still comply with Title 8.
- Municipal cemeteries often adhere to both local ordinances and state laws.

Common Issues and How to Avoid Them

Issue 1: Family Disputes

- When heirs disagree over rights, the Cemetery Authority should not take sides in the dispute.
- Require families to resolve disputes through succession documents or court orders and require those documents to be provided for the Cemetery Authority's records.

Issue 2: Double Sales

- Selling the same space twice is one of the most serious errors a cemetery can make.

- Avoid this by keeping accurate, updated plats and requiring staff to confirm availability before each sale.
- In the event such an unfortunate event happens, know the Cemetery Authority's right to correct errors, which allows a substitution if the substitution is approximately equal in value and location, so far as feasible:

§ 813. Correction of errors

A Cemetery Authority shall have the right to correct any and all errors that may occur in or in connection with the operation of the Cemetery, including without limitation those involving or in connection with the making of an interment, disinterment, or removal, or the description, transfer, granting the right of use, or conveyance of a cemetery space, and in this connection, the Cemetery Authority shall have the right to substitute, grant the right of use, or convey, in order to correct any such errors, other interment rights, approximately equal in value and location as far as feasible, as selected by the authority; or, in the sole discretion of the authority, the correction of an error may be accomplished by the refunding of the amount of money paid on account of the acquisition or use of a cemetery space. If an error involves an interment, the Cemetery Authority shall have the right to remove and transfer the remains that are involved. A Cemetery Authority shall have the right to correct any and all errors that may occur in or in connection with the operation of the Cemetery, including without limitation those involving or in connection with the making of an interment, disinterment, or removal, or the description, transfer, granting the right of use, or conveyance of a cemetery space, and in this connection, the Cemetery Authority shall have the right to substitute, grant the right of use, or convey, in order to correct any such errors, other interment rights, approximately equal in value and location as far as feasible, as selected by the authority; or, in the sole discretion of the authority, the correction of an error may be accomplished by the refunding of the amount of money paid on account of the acquisition or use of a cemetery space. If an error involves an interment, the Cemetery Authority shall have the right to remove and transfer the remains that are involved.

Issue 3: Incomplete Documentation

- Missing contracts or unrecorded transfers create long-term problems.
- Always make electronic backups of files and keep redundant copies of these backups to prevent documentation from going missing.
- Cemetery Authorities must establish a routine process for filing and verifying every transaction.

COMPLIANCE CHECKLIST

- ✓ Use written contracts with all required disclosures.
- ✓ Explain that families are purchasing interment rights, not the land itself.
- ✓ Deposit perpetual care funds from each sale promptly.
- ✓ Record all transfers and assignments in the Cemetery's official records.
- ✓ Maintain updated plats showing sold and unsold spaces.
- ✓ Provide families with copies of all documents.
- ✓ Train staff in both legal compliance and compassionate communication.
- ✓ Issue Titles or Deeds for the spaces within 30 days of receiving full payment.

CONCLUSION

Sales and conveyances form the foundation of cemetery operations. They provide revenue for the Cemetery, but more importantly, they establish the legal and emotional link between families and their loved ones' final resting places. By following Title 8's requirements and best practices, Cemetery Authorities can ensure every transaction is conducted with **integrity, transparency, and compassion**.

THE VOICE OF THE DEPARTED

GRAVE MATTERS
Personal Reflections of a Cemetery Director

As I mentioned previously, **La. R.S. 8:802(E)** allows the **Cemetery Authority** to **prevent a burial** in a space if someone **objects** and the cemetery believes the objection to be **reasonable**.

I once encountered a situation involving a **poorly written olographic affidavit** (that lacked proper form) from an individual claiming **rights of burial** in a space purchased by his now-deceased sister – a space that remained empty. He **did not possess the deed** or even a **copy of the written contract**.

As I began to research the matter, I discovered a **letter of protest** in the file, signed by the sister and sent through her **attorney**, stating that she was **estranged from her brother** and explicitly declared that, in the event of her death, **he was not permitted** to be buried in her space **under any circumstances**.

Based on that written protest, I had **no choice but to deny his request** for burial in that space. It was the only **credible, documented objection** from a person with legal standing. I explained that if he wished to challenge the objection, a **court order** would be required to **override the deceased's written wishes, as they** had no other living relatives. The matter quietly ended there; I never heard from him again.

The point I make here is that sometimes we must make **judgment calls** based on the **information available to us**. When a space owner's **intent is clear**, especially through a **written declaration**, my inclination is always to **honor those wishes**–unless and until a **judicial authority** directs otherwise.

CHAPTER 7

ABANDONED CEMETERY SPACES

Cemeteries are intended as permanent resting places, yet not every interment space sold will ultimately be used. Families may relocate, heirs may die without successors, or record-keeping may fail to keep pace with changing generations. Over time, large numbers of unused and largely forgotten cemetery plots can hinder a Cemetery Authority's ability to plan, maintain, and allocate space responsibly. Recognizing this reality, **Louisiana law provides a carefully regulated process for reclaiming "abandoned cemetery spaces."**

Statutory Framework

1. **Statewide definition** (outside New Orleans): A space is deemed **abandoned** if **either:**
    - **(C)(1)(a)** the Cemetery "has been unable to locate any of the owners or their successors or heirs **after diligent efforts for twenty-five (25) years," or**
    - **(C)(1)(b)** the space is **no longer fit for human burial**, there has been **no interment in the preceding 25 years, and** the Cemetery is unable to locate owners/heirs to provide care **after diligent efforts for one (1) year.**
2. **City of New Orleans** (municipal, religious, nonprofit cemeteries only): If a space has been **abandoned as defined in (C) for more than 10 years**, after advertising in the city's official journal, the Cemetery may **take possession (but not demolish)** and sell/convey under its rules.

What "Diligent Efforts" Require

A cemetery is **deemed** to have exercised "diligent efforts" only if it completes **all** of the following:

1. **Newspaper advertisements** (proposed acquisition notice):
    - For the **25-year track**: publish **once per year** in **each of the first 24 years, and once per month during the 25th year**.
    - For the **1-year track**: publish **once per month during that one year**.
2. **On-site posting:** Post a notice on the space once per month during the last year **of the a**pplicable period.
3. **Mailing:** Send a **registered or certified letter** to the **last known owner(s)** with the same notice (if name/address exists in the Cemetery's records).
4. **Court confirmation (if litigated):** A court may determine that diligent efforts were made, but only after the Cemetery demonstrates that it has completed the **one year of monthly ads, postings, and mailings** required at the end of the applicable period.

Note: The statute does **not indicate** that a plot being unused for 25 years is the same as being abandoned. Instead, it notes 25 years of documented inability to locate owners/heirs (through advertisements, postings, and mail).

Effect of Abandonment: Sale/Reuse

Once the conditions above are met, the space is **deemed abandoned**, and the Cemetery Authority may take action to sell or convey the space in accordance with its rules and conveyance procedures outlined in Title 8 (e.g., **La. R.S. 8:308(A)**). The New Orleans 10-year provision adds a possession step and prohibits demolition. Keep thorough proofs of publications, postings, and mailings.

COMPLIANCE CHECKLIST

25-Year Track – Unable to Locate Owners/Heirs (La. R.S. 8:308(C)(1)(a))

- ✓ Maintain a running file of **annual ads**, published once each year for years 1-24, stating the intent to acquire the space under **La. R.S. 8:308.**
- ✓ In **year 25**, publish **monthly ads** (12 total).
- ✓ **Post on space monthly** during year 25.
- ✓ **Mail a registered/certified** notice to the last known owner(s), if any record exists.
- ✓ After completing the 25 years, proceed (and, if court involvement is sought, present proof to satisfy **La. R.S. 8:308308(C)(2)(c)).** `

1-Year Track – Space Unfit; No Interment in Prior 25 Years (La. R.S. 8:308(C)(1)(b))

- ✓ Document the condition rendering the space unfit for human burial and the absence of interment for the prior 25 years.
- ✓ Publish monthly ads for 12 months stating the intent to acquire under La. R.S. 8:308.
- ✓ Post on the space monthly during that same 12-month period.
- ✓ Mail registered/certified notice to last known owner(s), if on record.
- ✓ After the 12th month, proceed (and present proofs if seeking judicial confirmation).

New Orleans (La. R.S. 8:308(B))

- ✓ If the space has been **abandoned under La. R.S. 8:308 (C) for less than 10 years**, publish in the city's official journal, and the Cemetery **may take possession (not demolish) and sell/convey** under **La R.S. 8:308(A)** rules. Keep proof of publication.

CONCLUSION

Abandonment under **La. R.S. 8:308** hinges on documented diligence, not mere non-use. Use the **25-year track when owners/heirs cannot be found over time; use the 1-year** track only when the space is **unfit,** and there has been **no interment in 25 years**. Follow the **ad/post/mail cadence** precisely and retain proofs for administrative and judicial review.

GRAVE MATTERS
Personal Reflections of a Cemetery Director

WHEN FOREVER GOES UNVISITED

Every cemetery director eventually faces the challenge of abandoned burial spaces. In today's digital world, it can feel outdated to require a 25-year search before declaring a space abandoned – and in some cases, it probably is. I've encountered situations where individuals purchased more spaces than they needed, failed to designate who was to be buried there, and passed away without any identifiable heirs. In such clear-cut cases, it seems reasonable to shorten the process for declaring a space abandoned.

Still, the law reflects a deep respect for family rights and lineage. Louisiana's cemetery statutes ensure that descendants have the opportunity to claim interment rights purchased by their ancestors. While our ability to locate heirs has improved significantly since these laws were enacted in 1974, we remain bound–both legally and ethically–to conduct diligent searches and follow established procedures for abandoned property.

CHAPTER 8

BURYING THE DEAD: BALANCING LEGAL REQUIREMENTS WITH A WORK OF MERCY

Burying the dead is one of humanity's oldest obligations, a duty rooted in respect, faith, and community. In Louisiana, this duty is also shaped by law. Title 8 provides detailed procedures to ensure that burials are conducted with dignity, order, and protection for families.

This chapter examines the legal procedures for burial outlined in Title 8 and explains how cemeteries, families, and the state collaborate to protect both the deceased and the living.

The Right of Interment

The foundation of any burial is the **interment right.** Unlike real estate purchase, this right does not grant ownership of land – it grants the right to be buried in a designated space. This fact cannot be emphasized enough, which is why it is mentioned repeatedly in this handbook, as it is the most common misunderstanding in cemeteries.

KEY POINTS:

- Interment rights must be recorded in the Cemetery's official records.
- When the purchaser dies, the right usually passes to heirs unless otherwise assigned.
- Cemeteries must respect the lawful holder of the right, even in cases of family disagreement.

This framework ensures burials occur only with proper authority, preventing confusion or unauthorized use of burial spaces.

PREPARING FOR BURIAL

Before a burial can occur, several procedural steps must be followed:

- **Verification of Rights**: The Cemetery must confirm that the family has a valid interment right. This is typically accomplished by the family presenting the deed or, if there is no deed, providing a contract indicating that all fees have been paid.
- **Burial Permit**: A burial transit permit, issued by the state or parish registrar, must be presented before interment.
- **Compliance with Cemetery Rules**: Cemeteries may impose requirements about vaults, markers, or memorials, provided these rules are consistent with Title 8.
- **Interment Orders**: If the person being buried is not the owner but is being buried with the owner's permission, have the owner sign an interment order granting permission for the burial. If the person ordering the interment is an heir rather than the original owner, having the individual execute a properly notarized Affidavit of Heirship can help alleviate many problems, especially

if other family members object to the interment afterward. Having an affidavit in place protects the Cemetery Authority from liability in **La. R.S. 8:804,** which gives the Cemetery the ability to rely on such for interment:

> **§ 804. Affidavit as authorization**
> In the absence of a formal judgment of possession in the succession of the record owner of a cemetery space or right of interment, an affidavit by a disinterested but informed person of the facts setting forth the fact of the death of the record owner and identifying the spouse and legal heirs of the decedent shall be complete and sufficient authorization for a Cemetery Authority to permit the use of any unoccupied portion of a cemetery space by the person or persons entitled to the use thereof.

Rights of Interment of Co-Owners

Co-owners of a burial space have a vested right to interment in any unoccupied space when such exists. For example, if a double mausoleum vault is purchased and owned by a husband and wife, both have the right to be interred in those spaces. The same would hold if two siblings were listed as co-owners on a contract/deed:

> **§ 806. Rights of co-owners**
> When the record title to a cemetery space or right of interment is in the names of two or more persons, each shall be considered as having a vested right therein and no conveyance or other disposition of space or right shall be recognized without the written concurrence of each record owner, but each owner shall have the right of interment in any unoccupied portion of the cemetery space at the time of death.

CEMETERY AUTHORITY'S RESPONSIBILITY:

No interment should take place without documentation verifying both the right of interment and the proper burial transit form.

OVERSEEING BURIALS

The act of burial itself is simple but highly regulated. Title 8 provides that:

- Cemeteries must maintain orderly burial practices that are consistent with their plats and maps.
- A register of burials must be maintained, recording the name of the deceased, the date of interment, and the location.
- Families must be given access to visit burial spaces after interment.

Regarding the last bullet point above, it is important to note that the right to visit burial spaces is not absolute. The Cemetery Authority does have the right to regulate the behavior of persons within the Cemetery in accordance with **La. R.S. 8:204(6)**. The Cemetery maintains the right under this provision to remove those who disturb the peace or who violate the rules and regulations of the Cemetery.

In Louisiana's Catholic tradition, burial is often accompanied by graveside services, including the Rite of Committal and the blessing of the grave. However, the legal framework applies equally to secular and non-religious cemeteries.

Record-Keeping and Documentation

Every burial must be recorded. Title 8 requires cemeteries to maintain:

- A **burial register** listing each interment.
- Updated **plats and maps** showing occupied and unoccupied spaces.
- Copies of all **permits, contracts, and consents** associated with the burial.

These records serve both practical and legal purposes. For families, they ensure that loved ones are properly memorialized. For the Cemetery, they protect against disputes and fulfill state inspection requirements.

Respect for Families and Traditions

Title 8 recognizes Louisiana's diverse religious and cultural traditions. Whether it is the Catholic practice of blessing graves on All Souls' Day, Protestant memorial services, or family-led rituals, the law provides flexibility — so long as basic procedural safeguards are met.

Cemeteries are encouraged to respect these practices while maintaining compliance with state law.

COMPLIANCE CHECKLIST

For Cemetery Authorities and cemetery staff, the following checklist ensures compliance with Title 8:

- ✓ Confirm interment rights with proper documentation.
- ✓ Verify the state-issued burial transit permit.
- ✓ Assign and mark the specific burial space on the cemetery plat.
- ✓ Record the burial in the Cemetery's official register.
- ✓ File and store all supporting documents (contracts, permits, consents).
- ✓ Ensure ongoing family access to the burial site.

Burying the dead in Louisiana is not only a matter of faith and tradition, but it is also a matter of law. Title 8 provides a clear, protective framework that ensures burials are conducted with dignity, order, and accountability.

By following these procedures, cemeteries honor both the living and the dead, carrying out one of humanity's oldest duties in a way that reflects Louisiana's enduring respect for sacred ground.

Conclusion

The act of burial represents one of society's oldest and most enduring duties – a final gesture of respect toward those who have died. In Louisiana, this responsibility carries both emotional and legal significance. Title 8 provides the structure that ensures every interment is conducted with dignity, clarity, documentation, and accountability, protecting families, Cemetery Authorities, and the integrity of the burial grounds themselves.

For the Cemetery Authority, each burial is not merely an operational event but a matter of trust. By verifying rights of interment, maintaining accurate records, and adhering to established procedures, the Cemetery fulfills its dual role: to serve the public faithfully and to safeguard the orderly preservation of every resting place.

When performed in accordance with both law and its sacred character, burial becomes more than an administrative process; it becomes a meaningful act of human decency and respect. In honoring the dead through proper care, we affirm the enduring values of respect, order, and responsibility that bind communities across generations.

GRAVE MATTERS
Personal Reflections of a Cemetery Director

MEMENTO MORI

The Latin phrase **"Memento Mori"** reminds us to always **keep death before us.** Caring for the dead is not merely a **duty**, but a **privilege**. We are **allowed to care** for those who have gone before us. **Where they are now, we shall one day be.**

As a Catholic Deacon, I also have the privilege of **presiding over burial rites** for many who pass through the gates of my cemetery for the last time. In addition to helping families make **final arrangements** for their loved ones, I accompany them in their **final acts of faith, commending their souls to Almighty God.**

As those entrusted with **managing cemeteries**, we make mistakes – I've certainly made my fair share during my tenure. The key is that we **learn from those mistakes.** Many times, those errors arise from a **lack of knowledge** or from navigating the **complex responsibilities** of cemetery management.

It's easy to let the daily routines – **maintaining property, installing plaques, entering burial records, posting obituaries, issuing permits** – become our primary focus. In reality, these are the **"busy work"** of our ministry – the operational necessities that support it, but are not the **heart of our vocation.** When we are suddenly bombarded with multiple **burial requests**, it can be overwhelming, and we may wonder how we will accomplish it all.

But the truth is this: **all of these things take a back seat** when it comes to **serving grieving families.** This must remain the **primary focus** of our work. Families turn to us in their **deepest sorrow,** relying on our **compassion, experience,** and **guidance** to help them navigate their loss.

When the first words I hear are, *"I'm calling because my wife died last night,"* or *"Mom passed away after a long illness,"* I remind myself that my role must shift – from administrative to **pastoral**, from process to **presence.** My work at that moment is not to type, but to **listen, comfort**, and **help carry the weight** of another person's grief.

We all fail at times, but we must **learn from failure**. I've learned not to assume that families understand what we in the cemetery profession consider "routine." To avoid miscommunication, I created **Standard Operating Procedures (SOPs)** for every type of interment in our cemetery.

In **South Louisiana**, for example, **ground burials** are often delayed – not by snow or ice, but by **rain** or **contractor availability.** As part of my process, I explain these circumstances in advance, provide a **written disclaimer**, and have families **sign** to confirm they understand. This small step has brought remarkable clarity and peace for families who might otherwise feel uncertain or frustrated.

When we **keep families informed** – explaining what is happening and why – I have found they are **more patient, more understanding**, and more grateful for our transparency.

We do well, then, to **evaluate our procedures**, **refine our processes**, and ensure that everything we do reflects **integrity**, **clarity**, and **pastoral care.** In doing so, we honor the sacred charge entrusted to us: to **serve the living**, by **reverently caring for the dead.**

CHAPTER 9

RECORDS & DOCUMENTATION STANDARDS

Under Chapter 9 of the LCB's regulations, every cemetery authority – whether operating under a certificate of authority or not – is required to maintain a full and accurate set of records documenting the cemetery's operations, history, and business.

What Must Be Maintained

The regulation mandates that records include, at a minimum: deeds, contracts, titles, certificates of interment rights; reports; accounting records and ledgers; maps, plats, and cemetery-space ownership records; interment and burial records; both current and historic price lists; any rules or regulations of the cemetery; and trust records – as well as any electronic records generated.

This broad coverage ensures not only that current operations are traceable but also that the historical record of ownership, interments, and institutional changes is preserved.

Transfer of Records Upon Change of Ownership or Control

When a cemetery is sold, or control passes to a new owner/authority, all of the records described above must be provided to the transferee. (cf. **La. Admin. Code tit. 46, XIII - §907)**

In practice, this means that no sale or transfer of a cemetery should proceed without a legally safeguarded "paper trail" (or electronic equivalent) — preserving institutional memory, protecting purchaser and purchaser's heirs, and preventing loss or obfuscation of burial, title, and trust-fund records.

Access by the Board and Oversight Authority

All records must be made available for inspection by the LCB at any time during regular business hours — either on-site at the cemetery or at another location designated by the Board. (cf. **La. Admin. Code tit. 46, XIII - §905)**

This requirement underpins regulatory oversight, allowing LCB to verify compliance, investigate complaints or disputes (e.g., about interments, trust funds, or ownership), and protect the public interest in the perpetual care and integrity of cemeteries.

Record Retention / Permanency Requirements

Chapter 9 distinguishes among different types of records for purposes of retention:

- Some records must be **permanently preserved** – among them: contracts and deeds, titles, certificates of interment rights; cemetery-space ownership records; interment/burial records; maps and plats; and the cemetery's current and historic rules/regulations. (cf. **La. Admin. Code tit. 46, XIII - §903(B)(1)**)
- Other records – such as accounting records, trust records, ledgers, annual reports, electronic backups, and price lists – must be retained for at least **seven years**, unless the Board otherwise directs. (cf. **La. Admin. Code tit. 46, XIII - §903(B)(2)**)
- Electronic records are acceptable, provided they are reproducible in a legible format, are accessible for review by the Board, and – upon request – can be printed out by the cemetery authority at its own expense. (cf. **La. Admin. Code tit. 46, XIII - §903(C)**)
- In addition, original (or "master") records – especially those concerning ownership, interments, and maps/plots – must be safeguarded against destruction (e.g., by fire) through duplicate copies stored off-site or by storing originals in a fireproof container. (cf. **La. Admin. Code tit. 46, XIII - §903(D)**)

Written Contracts & Sales Recording

When a cemetery sells interment rights, or cemetery-related merchandise or services, the transaction must be documented by a written contract. That contract must be clear and understandable, sequentially numbered, and entered in a sales journal.

As discussed in Chapter 6, each contract must include: the date, seller's and purchaser's names, identification of the cemetery space or interment rights, itemized pricing (including discounts), terms of payment, and — where applicable — disclosure of whether perpetual care applies; whether opening/closing is included; and how much (or what percentage) of the payment is placed into the cemetery's care or merchandise trust funds. (cf. **La. Admin. Code tit. 46, XIII -§909(C)**)

Contracts for cemetery merchandise or services must also describe the item or service in sufficient detail — including size, design, materials — and state the price and any trust-fund obligations for retained merchandise.

Why These Rules Matter

As you build educational materials and compliance checklists for cemetery authorities, notaries, attorneys, and families — especially within Louisiana's unique burial culture — these record-keeping requirements are fundamental. They safeguard interment rights over generations; they protect purchasers (and heirs) from loss, fraud, or erasure of documentation; they preserve institutional history (e.g., ownership changes, pricing over time, cemetery rules); and they enable regulatory accountability — especially for perpetual-care funding, trust-fund management, and interment integrity.

For example:

- In a deep-South, above-ground, multi-generation tomb culture, accurate maps/plots and interment records prevent misplaced burials or "lost tombs."
- Written, numbered contracts help protect families purchasing burial spaces — ensuring clarity as to what was included (space, perpetual care, opening/closing costs), and securing trust-fund contributions.
- Permanent preservation of deeds, titles, and interment rights supports future title transfers, inheritance, and family legacy — especially important in contexts of generational burials or family mausoleums.

- Retention of historic price lists and rules/regulations helps document how the cemetery's operation evolved over time — which can be vital for audits, legal disputes, or cultural heritage studies.

COMPLIANCE CHECKLIST

For Cemetery Authorities and cemetery staff, the following checklist ensures compliance with Title 8:

Permanent Records (Must Be Preserved Indefinitely)

La. Admin. Code tit. 46, XIII - §903(B)(1)

- ✓ Deeds, titles, and certificates of interment rights
- ✓ All contracts for the sale of interment rights
- ✓ Cemetery maps, plats, and space-ownership records
- ✓ Interment and burial records (including dates, locations, and decedent information)
- ✓ Historical and current cemetery rules and regulations
- ✓ Records of any transfers of ownership or control of the cemetery
- ✓ Any amendments or modifications to cemetery rules, ownership, or operation
- ✓ Master copies of documents governing the cemetery's dedication and perpetual servitude of use

Minimum 7-Year Retention Records

La. Admin. Code tit. 46, XIII - §903(B)(2)

- ✓ Accounting records and ledgers
- ✓ Annual reports required by the LCB
- ✓ Merchandise and service contracts (non-interment-right contracts)
- ✓ Price lists and fee schedules (including historical versions)
- ✓ Trust-fund accountings, statements, and deposits
- ✓ Sequential contract registers or sales journal

- ✓ Copies of all trust-fund deposit documentation for merchandise, services, and perpetual care
- ✓ Correspondence or notices related to payments, delinquencies, or cancellations
- ✓ Electronic records or backups (if not classified as permanent above)

Record Storage & Preservation Requirements
La. Admin. Code tit. 46, XIII - §903(D)

- ✓ Permanent records stored in a **fireproof cabinet**, vault, or protected facility
- ✓ Backups or duplicate copies maintained **off-site** or digitally secured
- ✓ Maps, plats, and interment records stored in a durable format resistant to damage
- ✓ Electronic records must be capable of being printed, reproduced, and provided to the LCB upon request
- ✓ Ensure no permanent record is deleted, overwritten, or

Conclusion

Accurate, complete, and accessible records are the backbone of every well-governed cemetery in Louisiana. Chapter 9 of the Louisiana Administrative Code makes clear that cemetery records are not merely internal administrative tools; they are legal instruments that safeguard interment rights, document contractual obligations, protect perpetual-care funds, and preserve the historical and cultural identity of a cemetery for generations. Whether a cemetery is privately owned, church-affiliated, or municipally operated, the duty to maintain permanent records is fundamental to public trust and regulatory compliance.

For cemetery authorities, these requirements are not burdensome formalities but essential practices of stewardship. They ensure continuity during changes in management or ownership, provide clarity for families navigating burial rights, and allow the Louisiana Cemetery Board to carry out its oversight responsibilities effectively. In a state where burial traditions are deeply woven into our cultural and religious life, proper documentation is a matter not only of law but of respect for the dignity of the dead and the rights of the living.

By establishing reliable, consistent systems for record preservation — whether through fire-protected storage, digital archiving, or standardized contract procedures — cemetery authorities honor the sacred trust placed in them. Robust records protect families from uncertainty, prevent disputes, and preserve the integrity of the cemetery's mission. In this way, compliance with Chapter 9 is more than regulatory adherence; it is an essential expression of the cemetery's commitment to transparency, continuity, and reverence for the generations who have gone before us.

CHAPTER 10

DISINTERMENTS AND REINTERMENTS

Of all cemetery operations, few tasks are as sensitive – or as legally regulated – as the removal and reburial of human remains. Known as disinterment (removal) and reinterment (reburial in a new location), these procedures touch the deepest concerns of families and the strongest protection of law.

Louisiana Revised Statutes Title 8 establishes strict rules for when and how disinterments may occur. As a Cemetery Authority, you must approach each request with compassion, caution, and compliance.

Legal Framework

Title 8 protects the sanctity of the grave by requiring one of two authorizations before disinterment:

Court Order

- A judge may issue an order permitting disinterment, often in cases involving public works projects, legal disputes, or contested rights.
- The Cemetery must receive and file a certified copy of the order before proceeding.

Written Family Consent

In most cases, disinterment requires written authorization from the decedent's next of kin.

- Louisiana law recognizes a hierarchy of relatives (spouse, adult children, parents, siblings, etc.) to determine who has authority.
- Title 8 requires that the majority of the nearest heirs must consent to the disinterment. For example, in the case of a child, **BOTH** parents would need to consent to such an interment. In the case of a person with children but no spouse, the majority of the children would need to provide consent. If the majority of the heirs do not consent, then a court order of the district court would be required to allow the disinterment and reinterment:

§ 659. Permission to move remains

A. The remains of a deceased person may be moved from a cemetery space to another cemetery space in the same cemetery or to another cemetery with the consent of the Cemetery Authority and the written consent of one of the following, in the order named, unless other specific directions, in the form of a notarial testament or a written and notarized declaration, have been given by the decedent:

(1) The surviving spouse, if there is no pending petition for divorce filed by either spouse prior to the death of the decedent spouse.

(2) A majority of the surviving adult children of the decedent.

(3) A majority of the surviving adult grandchildren of the decedent.

(4) The surviving parents of the decedent.

(5) A majority of the surviving adult siblings of the decedent.

B. If the required consent cannot be obtained, a final judgment of the district court of the parish where the Cemetery is situated shall be required.

WHY THIS MATTERS:

In the past, remains were sometimes moved without notice, leading to outrage and mistrust. Title 8 now protects families by ensuring that no one can disturb a grave without legal authority. This process also protects the Cemetery, so that the legal party with the rights to make such decisions is indeed the one requesting disinterment and reinterment.

CEMETERY AUTHORITY'S DUTY:

Never authorize the removal of remains without one of these legal foundations. Doing so exposes the Cemetery to liability and regulatory penalties.

Note: If the interment and disinterment is from one cemetery to another, then a licensed funeral director is required to oversee the disinterment and reinterment. If the disinterment and reinterment occur within the **SAME** cemetery, **La. R.S. 37:848** provides that the Cemetery sexton may supervise the disinterment and reinterment:

La. R.S. 37:848(A). Unlawful practice
No person, not certified and registered under the provisions of this Chapter, shall embalm, or pretend to practice the science of embalming, or conduct the business of funeral directing; however, a licensed funeral director shall not be required to supervise the disinterment of a dead human body when disinterment and reburial is made in the same cemetery by its designated sexton who shall be responsible to supervise the disinterment and reburial.

Although not required by law, if a cemetery sexton oversees such a disinterment and reinterment, it is advisable to have a form indicating the details of the disinterment/reinterment, signed by the sexton to memorialize the event.

Practical Procedures

Step 1: **Verify Authority**

- **Confirm** whether a court order or proper family consent backs the request.
- **Obtain notarized documents**, such as affidavits of heirship, to avoid disputes.

Step 2: **Documentation**

- **Secure the state-issued disinterment permit**, typically obtained through the parish registrar of vital records.
- **File copies of all supporting documents** (court order, consents, permits) in the Cemetery's permanent records.

Step 3: **Scheduling and Preparation**

- **Coordinate** with the funeral director, vault company, and, if required, public health officials.
- **Ensure proper equipment and staff are available** for safe and respectful handling.

Step 4: **Supervision of Removal**

- The cemetery sexton **must** be present to oversee the process.
- Remains **must** be treated with dignity, placed in a suitable container, and transported in accordance with Louisiana Department of Health regulations.

Step 5: **Reinterment**

- Once the new burial space is **confirmed**, proceed with reinterment.
- **Update cemetery plats**, burial registers, and interment records to reflect the change.

Special Situations

Public Necessity

Occasionally, cemeteries are affected by public projects (such as road construction or flood control). In such cases:

- Government agencies must follow the court order process.
- Cemeteries must work closely with officials to ensure compliance and notify families promptly and accurately.

Abandoned or Neglected Cemeteries

In rare cases, disinterment may occur as part of relocating remains from an abandoned or endangered cemetery. These cases require heightened oversight and community communication.

Religious Cemeteries

Church-operated cemeteries may have additional internal rules regarding disinterments, but these cannot override the requirements of Title 8.

Record-Keeping

For every disinterment and reinterment, cemeteries **must keep**:

- A copy of the court order **or** family consent (interment order).
- The disinterment permit.
- A record of the removal, including date, name of deceased, and new burial location.
- Updated plats showing the vacated and new interment spaces.

Tip: Treat disinterment files as permanent legal records.

Cemetery Authority's Role in Family Care

Disinterments are often emotionally charged. Families may request them for reasons ranging from relocation to family unity (e.g., moving remains to a family plot).

Best Practices:

- Meet with families personally to explain the process.
- Be transparent about costs and timelines.
- Emphasize that the law protects their loved one's dignity.
- Encourage legal resolution if disagreements arise between relatives.

COMPLIANCE CHECKLIST

- ✓ Obtain a court order or proper family consent.
- ✓ Secure a disinterment permit from the La. Dept. of Vital Statistics or Parish Coroner.
- ✓ Document and file all legal authorizations.
- ✓ Coordinate with funeral professionals and, if required, health officials.
- ✓ Supervise removal to ensure dignity and safety.
- ✓ Complete reinterment in the authorized location.
- ✓ Update cemetery plats and burial registers.
- ✓ Maintain permanent records of all proceedings.

CASE STUDY: *SONNIER V. FOUNDATION OF THE DIOCESE OF LAFAYETTE*

The modern case of *Sonnier v. Foundation of the Diocese of Lafayette* illustrates how Louisiana courts strictly apply **La. R.S. 8:659**, the statute governing the disinterment and reinterment of human remains.

Facts and Dispute: Eugene "Trey" Sonnier III, an Air Force servicemember, died in 2013. Prior to his death, he executed Department of Defense Form DD-93, designating his father as the **Person Authorized to Direct Disposition (PADD)** of his remains. Following Trey's death, his father arranged burial at Calvary Cemetery in Lafayette and purchased the interment space. Conflict arose when the Cemetery reissued the title jointly to both parents, and Trey's mother acquired adjoining plots. The father, believing his authority as PADD extended beyond the initial burial, sought to **disinter and reinter** Trey's remains elsewhere.

Court's Analysis: The Louisiana Supreme Court dismissed claims for ownership and damages but recognized that the father's petition had raised an alternative ground for relief under **R.S. 8:659**. That statute requires **written consent of the Cemetery Authority** and the **statutorily designated next of kin** (spouse, children, parents, or siblings) before remains may be moved, unless the deceased has provided other written directions. The Court emphasized that even with PADD status, a parent cannot bypass these statutory procedures. Because the father had not alleged that he sought consent from the Cemetery or shown that such consent was wrongfully withheld, his pleadings were defective. The Court remanded, allowing him to amend his petition, but made clear that federal PADD designations do not override Louisiana's statutory scheme for disinterment.

Lesson: Sonnier confirms that **R.S. 8:659 provides the exclusive pathway for disinterment in Louisiana.** While families may believe succession rights or federal military designations give them unilateral control, courts require strict compliance with the statute's consent requirements. The case underscores the dual reality: burial rights are inheritable and respected, but disinterment is an extraordinary act that can occur only when both the **Cemetery Authority and the statutory family class** consent — or when a court, upon proper pleadings, authorizes it.

Conclusion

Disinterments and reinterments are not routine tasks — they are profound responsibilities. Title 8 ensures that no remains are moved without lawful authority, protecting families and preserving the sanctity of the grave.

For Cemetery Authorities, following these procedures is more than legal compliance; it is a matter of trust. By handling disinterments with care, transparency, and respect, you uphold the dignity of the dead and the confidence of the living.

GRAVE MATTERS
Personal Reflections of a Cemetery Director

WHEN FINAL ISN'T FINAL

During my time in cemetery management, I have supervised numerous **disinterments** and **reinterments** within my cemetery.

One such case involved a gentleman who had purchased **multiple burial spaces** and expressed the wish that, upon his death, his **wife be moved** from her original space and **reinterred beside him** in two adjoining spaces he had purchased. Fortunately, this was an easy matter to handle because he had the **foresight to visit a notary public** beforehand and **execute a notarial declaration** clearly stating his wishes.

The family requested that the **disinterment and reinterment occur on the same morning** as the gentleman's funeral, and that the **crypt door remain open**, making it a kind of **double funeral.** I was happy to accommodate this request – especially since the **casket was in remarkably good condition**, considering it was a **wooden casket** in the humid climate of **South Louisiana.**

On the morning of the funeral, which I had the **privilege to preside over**, the family was deeply moved to see the **matching caskets side by side** – husband and wife reunited, just as he had planned.

Of course, not every disinterment happens under such **favorable circumstances.** Some are required due to **autopsy orders, coroner investigations**, or other difficult situations. But in this instance, it was an honor to assist a man who wished only to **rest beside his beloved** in a space prepared for both.

As noted in this chapter, the **cemetery sexton** has the **legal authority under Louisiana law** to supervise disinterments and reinterments within his or her cemetery. Early in my tenure, I realized there was often **no paper trail** to memorialize these events. While not required by statute, I found it essential to **create documentation for posterity.**

To address this, I developed a **Cemetery Disinterment and Reinterment Record Form**, included in the **companion forms book** in this series. This form allows the sexton to **record all pertinent details** – dates, spaces involved, and the reason for movement – thereby creating an **internal record** of the process. I also ensure that all **supporting documents** authorizing the procedure are kept on file with the cemetery's records.

As a **notary public**, I notarize the form used for disinterment, though **no statute requires notarization.** The notarization simply reinforces the **integrity of the record**. This form is also available in the **Louisiana Cemetery Forms Book** for others to adopt in their own operations.

The key takeaway is simple: whenever something happens in the cemetery – a burial, a disinterment, or a reinterment – it must be **documented and preserved.** These records serve not only for **historical purposes** but also for the **efficiency and accuracy** of those who will one day follow in our footsteps.

When we keep careful records, we honor not just the **dead** we serve, but also the **future caretakers** who will inherit our work – and continue the sacred duty of maintaining the **integrity and memory of the resting place.**

CHAPTER II

PERPETUAL CARE VS. PARTICULAR CARE

Louisiana law requires cemeteries to provide for the long-term care of their grounds, distinguishing between two categories: perpetual care (also known as endowed care) and particular care (sometimes referred to as special care). These are addressed in Louisiana Revised Statutes Title 8 (Cemeteries), which outlines definitions, requirements, and protections for families.

As a Cemetery Authority, it is necessary to understand the obligations imposed by **La. R.S. 8:1**, **La. R.S. 8:451 - 467.1**, and related provisions to remain compliant.

DEFINITIONS

Perpetual or Endowed Care is defined in **La. R.S. 8:1(5)** as the maintenance, repair, and care of all places of interment, including improvements made upon them, in keeping with a well-maintained cemetery, together with general overhead expenses necessary for such purposes.

Care Funds are defined in **La. R.S. 8:1(6)** as all money held in trust under **La. R.S. 8:454** and **8:454.1**, including principal and income from investments, dedicated exclusively to perpetual care.

Perpetual Care Requirements

Trust Fund Mandate: La. R.S. 8:454 requires cemeteries that represent themselves as perpetual care cemeteries to establish and maintain a perpetual care trust fund. A portion of the proceeds from the sale of interment rights must be deposited into the fund.

Fund Management: The principal of the fund must remain intact; only income may be used for maintenance and upkeep **(La. R.S. 8:454(C))**. **La. R.S. 8:459.1** requires that if a cemetery changes ownership or becomes a religious, fraternal, or municipal cemetery, the trust fund remains in place and continues to be used solely for the care of the Cemetery.

Depositing of Funds: The Louisiana Administrative Code requires that collected perpetual care funds be deposited promptly. Specifically, funds must be deposited within 30 days after the close of the month in which they are collected:

La. Admin. Code tit. 46, XIII – 1501(D) – Payments to Perpetual Care Trust Fund

All perpetual or endowed care deposits shall be delivered to the trustee not later than the thirtieth day after the close of the month of the sale or transfer of the interment space or interment right by the Cemetery Authority or cemetery sales/management organization. However, if the sale or transfer is financed by the seller and payments are pursuant to an installment contract, then the deposits to the trust fund must be made either:

1. not later than the thirtieth day of the close of the month in which the contract is made; or
2. proportionally over the term of the contract, provided that the seller maintains adequate accounting records of the installment payments and the proportionate amounts due the trust.

Oversight: Records of perpetual care funds must be open for inspection under **La. R.S. 8:463.** The Louisiana Cemetery Board enforces compliance, including the submission of required reports and the maintenance of accounting records.

Items Covered by Perpetual Care

- Mowing, landscaping, and general groundskeeping.
- Repair and maintenance of roads, drainage, fences, and common structures.
- Upkeep of mausoleum exteriors and columbaria.
- Removal of trash and debris.
- General overhead related to cemetery maintenance.

Particular (Special) Care

Nature of Particular Care:

While not defined by statute, "particular care" is generally understood as special or individualized services contracted by a family for a specific grave, lot, crypt, or niche. The Perpetual Care Trust does not fund these services; instead, they are supported through direct payments under private agreements.

Items Covered by Particular Care:

- Planting or maintaining flowers or shrubs at a specific grave.
- Special cleaning, polishing, or preservation of a monument.
- Seasonal or holiday decorations.
- Interior maintenance of private mausoleums or crypts.

- Repairs or enhancements beyond standard upkeep, such as headstones, monuments, and markers.

KEY DIFFERENCES BETWEEN PERPETUAL AND PARTICULAR CARE

FEATURE	PERPETUAL CARE (La. R.S. 8:454)	PARTICULAR CARE
Legal Basis	Required if the Cemetery advertises perpetual care	Voluntary, contractual
Funding	Trust fund required; principal preserved, income used	Paid directly by family
Scope	Cemetery-wide upkeep and maintenance	Individual grave, lot, or structure
Oversight	Louisiana Cemetery Board, records open under **La. R.S. 8:463**	Cemetery's internal record-keeping
Examples	Mowing, fences, mausoleum exteriors	Flowers, monument cleaning, mausoleum interior care

CASE STUDY: *WESTLAWN CEMETERIES, LLC V. LOUISIANA CEMETERY BOARD*

Facts and Dispute: Westlawn Cemeteries, a private Cemetery Authority, challenged a Louisiana Board regulation found in **La. Admin. Code, Title 46, Part XIII, §1503(C)**. This rule restricted the disbursement of perpetual care trust funds, imposing additional requirements not contained in Title 8. Westlawn argued that the regulation exceeded the Board's statutory authority and unlawfully altered the Legislature's framework for managing trust funds.

Court's Analysis: The Louisiana Supreme Court struck down the rule, holding that the Board had exceeded its authority under **La. R.S. 8:67**. The Court reasoned that while the Board has power to enforce and administer Title 8, it cannot create substantive obligations or restrictions that conflict with or go beyond the statute itself. Because Title 8 already provides a comprehensive framework for perpetual care funds, the regulation was invalid.

Lesson: *Westlawn* underscores that Cemetery Authorities must look directly to Title 8 for their obligations. Administrative regulations cannot expand or contradict statutory provisions. For Cemetery Authorities, this case is a reminder that compliance rests on the law as written, not on unauthorized agency rules; for the Board, it serves as a warning that its regulatory powers are strictly bounded by statute.

COMPLIANCE CHECKLIST

- ✓ Establish and maintain perpetual care trust if required (La. R.S. 8:454).
- ✓ Deposit required amounts from interment rights sales into the trust.
- ✓ Preserve principal; use only income for upkeep.
- ✓ Maintain accurate records of care fund deposits and expenditures **(La. R.S. 8:463)**.
- ✓ Clearly explain to families what perpetual care covers and offer separate agreements for particular care.
- ✓ Train staff to avoid misrepresenting perpetual care as including specific care services.
- ✓ When determining whether an item is covered under perpetual care or particular care, determine whether the benefit applies to a single space holder or to a group of space holders. If it benefits only one individual, then it is most likely a particular care situation. However, if it benefits a group of spaces (such as an entire mausoleum or a section or row), then it is most likely covered under perpetual care.

CONCLUSION

Under Title 8, the concept of care extends far beyond immediate maintenance – it encompasses a continuing duty to preserve the Cemetery's physical and financial integrity. Perpetual care ensures the long-term maintenance of the Cemetery as a whole – its grounds, structures, and shared facilities – while particular care provides individualized attention to specific lots, crypts, or memorials as requested by families. Both are essential components of responsible cemetery management, and both carry binding legal obligations.

As the Cemetery Authority, you serve not merely as an administrator but as a trustee of public confidence and family trust. You are responsible for managing funds in a manner that honors donor intent, complies with statutory accounting requirements, and ensures that care continues long after individual memories have faded.

By maintaining clear distinctions between perpetual and particular care, and by safeguarding all funds in compliance with Louisiana law, **R.S. 8:901 et seq.**, and by enforcing transparent reporting and deposit practices, you uphold both the spirit and the letter of the law. In doing so, you protect your cemetery's reputation, strengthen community trust, and preserve the integrity of the grounds entrusted to your care for generations to come.

Ultimately, the careful administration of care funds is more than a financial duty – it is an act of stewardship. Through diligence, accountability, and foresight, the Cemetery Authority ensures that every promise made to a family today remains fulfilled tomorrow.

GRAVE MATTERS
Personal Reflections of a Cemetery Director

ROSES FOR MAMA

Besides the distinction between **interment rights** and **ownership of real property,** the most significant **misunderstanding** I often encounter with families is the **expectation of what "perpetual care" means** versus **particular care.**

I am reminded of a joke a **priest friend** once played on me during my early tenure as Cemetery Director. He called the office and said, "I'm calling to complain because I paid **$5 back in 1975**, and I was told a **rose would be placed on my grandmother's grave every week.**" Though clearly in jest, as with all good jokes, there was **truth behind the humor.**

That truth is this: we must be **clear and careful** when explaining the **difference between perpetual care and particular care. Perpetual care** refers to the **ongoing maintenance** of the **cemetery grounds**—mowing, trimming, road maintenance, and overall appearance. A simple way to remember it: *if it serves the* ***common good of all****, it falls under perpetual care.*

Families often believe that because they or the cemetery have **paid into perpetual care**, it means the cemetery is responsible for **cleaning, repairing, or restoring individual graves and memorials.** I've received more than a few calls from families asking when I would be **pressure washing their loved one's graves** because they "paid perpetual care." I always take the time to explain that **individual grave upkeep**—cleaning, decoration, or restoration—is the **responsibility of the family,** not the cemetery. I also remind them that **pressure washing** can cause damage and **raise liability concerns, and that gentle hand cleaning is the safer and** preferred method.

Because not all families have the time, resources, or physical ability to maintain these spaces, I established a **Particular Care Service** at our cemetery. This allows families to request **individual restoration or cleaning services** at a **nominal fee.** I have found that this program provides a **meaningful revenue stream** for the cemetery while also meeting a **pastoral need**—offering families peace of mind and preserving the **dignity of the resting place.**

The old joke also carries another lesson: we must be **faithful to the care agreements** we make. When a family pays for **flowers on holidays**, we ensure they are placed. When a family pays to have **plaques cleaned and sealed annually**, we make certain it is done. These are not just **business agreements**; they are **acts of mercy** for the **faithful departed** and **expressions of trust** between the cemetery and the families it serves.

For this reason, when entering into **particular care agreements**, we should always **clearly outline** the services to be provided, so families never feel **misled or disappointed.** Managing expectations is simple when we practice **clarity, transparency, and foresight**—and when we **put everything in writing.**

Above all, we must help families understand the **difference between perpetual care**—which sustains the **cemetery as a whole**—and **particular care**, which attends to the **individual resting places** entrusted to our care.

CHAPTER 12

CEMETERY RULES AND REGULATIONS

Every Cemetery must operate under a framework of rules and regulations that balance family rights, public health, religious traditions, and the orderly management of burial grounds. Title 8 recognizes cemetery operators' authority to establish rules while also protecting families from arbitrary or unreasonable restrictions.

This chapter outlines the legal foundation for cemetery rules under Title 8 and provides Cemetery Authorities with guidance on creating and enforcing regulations that are both compliant and compassionate.

Cemetery rules and regulations establish the framework for dignity, order, and safety within burial grounds. In Louisiana, the authority for adopting such rules is codified in the Louisiana Revised Statutes, Title 8, particularly **La. R.S. 8:204 - 206.**

The law grants Cemetery Authorities broad powers to regulate their cemeteries; however, principles of reasonableness and fairness limit these powers. Louisiana courts and the Attorney General have clarified that rules cannot be arbitrary, discriminatory, or contrary to Title 8.

Source of Authority

La. R.S. 8:204 provides that cemeteries have the duty, ability, and right to establish rules and regulations and to enforce such:

> **§ 204. Specific powers; rulemaking and enforcement**
> Every Cemetery Authority may make, adopt, amend, add to, revise, or abolish rules and regulations for the use, care, control, management, restriction, and protection of its Cemetery, and for regulating the placement, uniformity, class, and kind of markers, monuments, and other structures within the Cemetery, and to prevent interments in violation of law or of its rules and regulations.

This statute grants Cemetery Authorities broad discretion, including rules regarding hours, conduct, decorations, monuments, and other matters that affect the Cemetery's order and appearance.

Publication and Inspection of Rules

La. R.S. 8:205 provides the following guidelines regarding Cemetery Rules and Regulations:

> **§ 205. Rules and Regulations**
> The rules and regulations made pursuant to R.S. 8:204 shall be plainly printed or typewritten and maintained subject to inspection in the office of the Cemetery Authority.

Thus:

- Rules must be **written.**
- They must be **kept on file at the Cemetery's office.**
- They must be **open to public inspection.**

Contracts and Disclosure

La. R.S. 8:206 requires that there be written contracts that mention the Rules and Regulations of the Cemetery:

> **§ 206. Contracts required; disclosure**
> A Cemetery Authority offering to provide burial rights or a Cemetery Authority or other entity offering Cemetery related merchandise and services shall provide to the customer, upon purchase, a written contract which complies with the requirements set forth in this Title and the rules and regulations of the Louisiana Cemetery Board. This ensures that purchasers are bound by cemetery rules and that every contract explicitly incorporates them.

Rules and Vested Rights

Even after interment rights have vested, they remain subject to reasonable cemetery rules and regulations.

La. R.S. 8:811 provides that "The vested right of interment ... shall not authorize the owner to make any interment in violation of the rules and regulations of the Cemetery Authority." This underscores that interment rights are not absolute but must be exercised within the framework of published rules and regulations.

ATTORNEY GENERAL OPINION NO. 89 - 0565

The Louisiana **Attorney General's Opinion No. 89 - 0565** (1989) addressed what constitutes "reasonable" cemetery rules under Title 8.

This opinion provides practical guidance: a rule is enforceable **if it is:**

- Adopted in accordance with **La. R.S. 8:204 - 205.**
- Published and disclosed to purchasers.
- Reasonable, nondiscriminatory, and tied to a legitimate purpose (safety, uniformity, order, or preservation).

KEY POINTS:

- A Cemetery Authority may adopt rules that limit decorations, regulate monument types, or set hours of operation, provided that these rules are applied uniformly and serve a legitimate purpose, such as safety, order, or preservation.
- Rules must be reasonable, not arbitrary. For example:
    - A rule prohibiting glass containers to prevent breakage and injury would be considered reasonable.
    - A rule that selectively prohibited certain families from using particular decorations, while allowing others, would be discriminatory and unreasonable.

The Attorney General confirmed that the authority granted by Title 8 is broad, but principles of fairness and consistency always constrain it.

Practical Applications

- **Decoration Rules:** Cemeteries may prohibit breakable vases or balloons, provided this prohibition applies equally to all lots and is based on safety or grounds maintenance.
- **Monument Rules:** Authorities may restrict upright markers in certain sections for uniformity, provided the rule is clearly published and not selectively enforced.
- **Access Rules:** Visiting hours may be established for security purposes, but they must be consistent and reasonable.
- **Special Days:** Authorities may temporarily relax rules for cultural observances, such as All Saints' Day, provided those exceptions are clearly communicated.

COMPLIANCE CHECKLIST

- ✓ Adopt rules in writing under **La. R.S. 8:204.**
- ✓ Keep rules on file and available for inspection under **La. R.S. 8:205.**
- ✓ Ensure that sales contracts incorporate cemetery rules as outlined in **La. R.S. 8:206.**
- ✓ Apply all rules consistently and reasonably, per **AG Op. 89 - 0565.**
- ✓ Confirm that the rules do not conflict with statutory protections under Title 8.

CONCLUSION

Louisiana law grants Cemetery Authorities broad discretion to adopt rules and regulations, but reasonableness is the key principle under Louisiana law. **R.S. 8:204 – 206** and **Attorney General Opinion 89 - 0565** require that regulations be written, published, incorporated into contracts, and applied uniformly. They must serve legitimate purposes, such as safety, preservation, and order — never arbitrary control. By adhering to these standards, Cemetery Authorities not only comply with the law but also maintain trust with the families they serve.

GRAVE MATTERS
Personal Reflections
of a Cemetery Director

LAW AND ORDER

Enforcing cemetery rules and regulations is often one of the **most challenging aspects** of managing a cemetery. I find **rule enforcement** to be one of the **most demanding tasks** I face on a daily basis. I take **no pleasure** in removing items or telling a grieving family member that something they placed **isn't permitted.** Still, I remind myself that these actions are for the **common good**—to preserve the **dignity, order, and beauty** of the cemetery for all.

Early in my tenure, I encountered a situation where someone had **written a message on the granite of a mausoleum door.** The gesture was heartfelt but **inappropriate for sacred grounds.** Every cemetery has its own **rules and protocols**, but the key is this: once a policy is established, it must be **enforced fairly and consistently.**

I often explain to families that what is allowed for one must be allowed for all. **Cemetery policy must be universal.** When setting or reviewing rules, I ask myself: *"Would I be comfortable if every family did this on every space in the cemetery?"*

Though **everyone grieves differently**, one family's expression cannot come at the **expense of others' rights or peace.** Cemetery spaces are **sacred places of remembrance**, not **personal shrines** or **cookie-cutter landscapes.** The challenge—and the duty—of a Cemetery Director is to find the **balance between personal expression and collective reverence**, keeping the cemetery a place of **peace and shared beauty** for all who visit.

CHAPTER 13

MERCHANDISE TRUST FUNDS

In Louisiana, cemeteries that sell burial merchandise such as vaults, caskets, memorials, crypts, or niches before the time of need are subject to strict trust fund requirements. These safeguards, found in **La. R.S. 8:601 – 606 are designed to protect consumers by ensuring that money paid in advance for merchandise is** available when needed.

A Cemetery Authority must understand when merchandise trust fund requirements apply, what percentage must be deposited, and the categories of cemeteries that are exempt.

WHAT IS A MERCHANDISE TRUST FUND?

A merchandise trust fund is a legally required trust account into which a Cemetery Authority must deposit a percentage of the purchase price of burial merchandise that is sold in advance of need.

La. R.S. 8:601(A) requires that 70% of the purchase price of each item of merchandise sold for future delivery be deposited into the merchandise trust fund.

The principal and earnings remain in trust until the merchandise is delivered or installed.

Funds can only be withdrawn upon delivery and completion of installation, or upon lawful cancellation of the contract in accordance with its terms and conditions.

Purpose of the Fund

The merchandise trust fund ensures that:

- Families who pre-purchase vaults, markers, or crypts are guaranteed delivery, even if the Cemetery Authority faces financial hardship.
- Advance payments cannot be misused before obligations are fulfilled.
- The public has confidence in pre-need purchases.

Cemeteries Exempt from Merchandise Trust Fund Requirements

Not every Cemetery Authority is required to maintain a merchandise trust fund. **La. R.S. 8:601(B)** specifically exempts:

- **Religious cemeteries** owned and operated by a recognized church or religious order.
- **Fraternal cemeteries** operated by a recognized fraternal organization.
- **Municipal cemeteries** owned and operated by a municipality or political subdivision.
- **Community cemeteries** operated on a nonprofit basis for the benefit of a specific community.

Key Points:

Private, for-profit Cemetery Authorities that advertise or sell merchandise for pre-need delivery are not exempt and must comply fully with trust fund laws.

Record-keeping and Oversight

Cemetery Authorities **must maintain detailed records** of all deposits, contracts, and trust balances **(La. R.S. 8:603)**.

The Louisiana Cemetery Board has the authority to inspect records and enforce compliance with regulations.

Annual reports are required to demonstrate that funds have been properly deposited and administered.

Practical Guidance for Cemetery Authorities

Contracts: Sales contracts for merchandise must specify that funds will be deposited into the merchandise trust.

- **Deposits:** Deposit 70% of the purchase price promptly into the fund **(La. R.S. 8:601)**.
- **Withdrawals:** Permitted only after the merchandise has been delivered and installed.
- **Transparency:** Clearly explain to families that the merchandise trust protects their purchase until delivery is made.

- **Exemptions:** Confirm whether the Cemetery qualifies as exempt (religious, fraternal, municipal, or nonprofit community). If not, full compliance is mandatory.

COMPLIANCE CHECKLIST

- ✓ Deposit 70% of pre-need merchandise sales into a merchandise trust fund **(La. R.S. 8:601)**.
- ✓ Keep detailed records of deposits and balances **(La. R.S. 8:603)**.
- ✓ File annual reports with the Louisiana Cemetery Board.
- ✓ Allow inspections of trust records upon request.
- ✓ Do not withdraw funds until the merchandise is delivered and installed.
- ✓ Confirm whether the Cemetery qualifies as exempt.

Conclusion

Merchandise trust funds provide critical protection for families who plan ahead. **La. R.S. 8:601 - 606** requires that most Cemetery Authorities set aside 70% of pre-need merchandise sales in trust until delivery is made. However, **religious, fraternal, municipal, and nonprofit community cemeteries are exempt from this requirement.**

CHAPTER 14

LOUISIANA BURIAL TRADITIONS AND CULTURAL CONTEXT

Louisiana's cemetery law, as codified in Title 8, cannot be fully understood apart from the state's unique cultural, historical, and religious traditions. The statutes reflect not only the civil law heritage of Louisiana but also the profound influence of Catholicism, the practical realities of the Gulf South environment, and the customs of diverse communities that have lived and died here.

Catholic Influence in South Louisiana

The Catholic Church has played a defining role in Louisiana burial traditions. In Acadiana and throughout southern Louisiana, parish cemeteries remain central to community life. Catholic canon law emphasizes burial in consecrated ground, a principle that resonates with the perpetual dedication provisions of Louisiana law **(La. R.S. 8:304)**.

The concept of perpetual care **(La. R.S. 8:454 – 466)** reflects not only a financial mechanism but a theological conviction: that the dignity of the human body endures beyond death. Families expect cemeteries to maintain the sanctity of gravesites across generations, a responsibility that Cemetery Authorities fulfill both legally and pastorally.

The New Orleans Tomb Tradition

Perhaps the most famous expression of Louisiana burial culture is the above-ground tombs of New Orleans. Due to the high water table, early settlers found that ground burials were frequently disturbed by flooding. The response was the construction of elaborate masonry tombs and vaults, often serving entire families or societies.

These structures, now protected under the historic cemetery provisions **(La. R.S. 8:903–910)**, are more than functional — they are heritage monuments. Cemeteries like St. Louis No. 1 have become landmarks, reflecting the architectural styles and cultural identities of their time. Statutory protections against desecration and abandonment underscore the recognition of these cemeteries as part of Louisiana's patrimony.

African American Cemeteries

Throughout Louisiana, African American cemeteries bear witness to both struggle and resilience. Many were established by freedmen's communities after the Civil War, often on church grounds or donated land. Others are segregated sections within larger cemeteries.

Because some of these cemeteries lack formal perpetual care funds, they are especially vulnerable to neglect. Title 8's abandonment and removal provisions **(La. R.S. 8:304 – 312)** have sometimes been invoked to address such cemeteries. Increasingly, community groups and historical societies are working to preserve these sacred spaces, recognizing their role in telling the story of African American life in Louisiana.

Native American Burial Grounds

Long before European settlement, Native Americans buried their dead in Louisiana's soil. Mound sites and other burial grounds remain throughout the state. While not directly governed by Title 8, these sites fall under broader historic preservation and federal protection statutes. Their existence reminds Cemetery Authorities that burial practices in Louisiana date back far longer than the statutes that govern them.

Fraternal and Benevolent Societies

Louisiana also has a tradition of fraternal, benevolent, and mutual aid societies that established cemeteries. These organizations — such as the French, Italian, and African American societies of New Orleans — purchased and maintained collective tombs for their members. Statutes governing the powers of Cemetery Authorities (**La. R.S. 8:201 - 205**) apply to such organizations, ensuring they fulfill the same duties as other Cemetery Authorities.

Legal Reflections of Cultural Practices

Title 8 integrates these diverse traditions into a legal framework that ensures order, fairness, and respect. The dedication of cemetery lands **(La. R.S. 8:304)**, the regulation of disinterments **(La. R.S. 8:659)**, the oversight of perpetual care funds **(La. R.S. 8:454 - 466)**, and the recognition of historic cemeteries **(La. R.S. 8:903 - 910)** all bear witness to Louisiana's blending of law and culture.

Cemetery Authorities must therefore see themselves not only as administrators but as stewards of memory. By honoring these traditions, they fulfill both the letter of the law and the spirit of the communities they serve.

Conclusion

Louisiana's cemetery law is more than a technical body of statutes — it is a living reflection of the people who shaped it. The provisions of Title 8 codify centuries of belief in the dignity of the human person, the permanence of memory, and the sanctity of place. From the consecrated grounds of Catholic parishes to the tombs of New Orleans, from rural African American cemeteries to Native burial sites, each resting place tells part of the story of Louisiana's identity.

To interpret and apply these laws faithfully, Cemetery Authorities must therefore act not merely as custodians of property, but as guardians of heritage. Every burial, record, and act of maintenance participates in a tradition that unites faith, family, and law. In honoring that tradition, Louisiana fulfills both its legal duty and its moral inheritance — to preserve sacred ground as a testament to those who have gone before and a promise to those who will follow.

GRAVE MATTERS
Personal Reflections
of a Cemetery Director

SIX FEET AND A CENTURY DEEP

As a Catholic Deacon, I understand the importance of **honoring religious and cultural customs.** Being a **cemetery manager** has opened my eyes to **traditions from many faiths and cultures** that I had never encountered before.

As Catholics, we have the beautiful tradition of blessing graves on All Souls' Day, which is widely observed by families here in South Louisiana. As part of this tradition, it is customary to bring a **potted plant** to place at the graves of loved ones. Because I manage a **Catholic cemetery,** we **relax our general rules**—which normally **prohibit potted plants**—for **All Souls' Day and the week following**, recognizing that this practice is a **longstanding South Louisiana Catholic custom.**

Regardless of whether the cemetery you manage is secular or religious, I encourage you to relax your rules when appropriate to accommodate practices that hold **deep religious or cultural significance.** For example, it is common in **many Asian cultures** to place **incense pots** on graves. The **rising smoke** is believed to **carry prayers to ancestors, invite blessings**, and **symbolize the ongoing bond** between the living and the dead.

I recently spoke with a family about these incense pots and explained their **cultural significance** to my staff. I asked the family to **replace porcelain pots with metal ones**, which would be **safer and more durable**, and allowed us to **secure them permanently to the ledger.** The family was happy to oblige. That simple conversation built **mutual respect and understanding**, showing that we could **honor their traditions** while maintaining **safety and uniformity** within the cemetery.

I realize that such accommodations are **not always possible**, especially when certain practices **conflict with religious convictions**. For example, because I manage a **Catholic cemetery**, I cannot allow **symbols or rituals** that **directly contradict Catholic beliefs**. This is part of the **balance we must maintain**—recognizing that those who choose to be buried in a **Catholic cemetery** do so within the **context of Catholic teaching and sacred tradition**.

Ultimately, our goal as cemetery professionals is to **honor the dead, serve the living**, and **respect the faith and culture** that give meaning to both. By finding ways to **blend compassion with consistency**, we preserve what is sacred—not only in our grounds, but in the hearts of those we serve.

CHAPTER 15

ABANDONMENT AND REMOVAL OF DEDICATION

Under **La. R.S. 8:304**, dedication of land for cemetery purposes does not transfer ownership, but it imposes a **permanent restriction** limiting the land's use to burial and memorial purposes. Once dedicated, the property becomes **cemetery land in perpetuity**, protected by both statute and public policy.

The servitude of use preserves the rights of interment-space owners and their families, ensuring that sacred ground cannot be sold, developed, or otherwise used without following the formal legal process for removal of dedication.

ABANDONED CEMETERIES

Chapter 6-A of Title 8 governs **abandoned cemeteries**, meaning entire burial grounds for which ownership cannot reasonably be determined or located.

La. R.S. 8:411(1) defines what is considered an abandoned cemetery:

> § 411. Definitions
> (1) "Abandoned cemetery" means any cemetery for which the board, in its discretion and after having been provided with the requisite title information establishing the title owner of the property, determines it is impossible or impractical to locate the current owner based upon its findings, including but not limited to a presentation of title history by the applicant for an abandoned cemetery sales and management license.

Sections **8:412 – 418** provide for:

- Licensing of **nonprofit entities** to operate or manage abandoned cemeteries **(La. R.S. 412 – 414)**;
- Regulation of sales, maintenance, and public health concerns **(La. R.S. 415 – 416)**;
- Procedures when **human remains or unmarked graves are discovered (La. R.S. 417)**; and
- Clarification that these provisions do not override other parts of Title 8 **(La. R.S. 418)**.

These statutes ensure that cemeteries without identifiable owners remain subject to lawful management, respectful maintenance, and state oversight.

ABANDONED INTERMENT SPACES

By contrast, **La. R.S. 8:308** addresses *abandoned interment spaces*—individual graves, vaults, or crypts within an active cemetery. When an interment space has not been used, maintained, or claimed for a statutory period and reasonable efforts to contact the owner or heirs have been unsuccessful, the cemetery authority may petition the district court for permission to reclaim and resell that individual space.

This statute applies to **isolated, unused spaces**, not to the cemetery as a whole.

REMOVAL OF DEDICATION OF CEMETERY LAND

The **removal of dedication** is a distinct process from abandonment.

Under **La. R.S. 8:306 - 307**, only a **district court** may authorize the removal of dedication of cemetery land. The court must ensure:

1. **Notice to interested parties** – including heirs, lot owners, and descendants;
2. **Respectful disposition of human remains** – with disinterment and reinterment in another lawful cemetery under **La. R.S. 8:659**; and
3. **Preservation or relocation of monuments and markers** – to ensure dignity and historical continuity.

Only after the court finds that continued cemetery use is **impossible or impractical**, and after all remains are lawfully reinterred, may the dedication be removed and the land revert to non-cemetery use.

Public Policy Considerations

Louisiana's cemetery laws reflect a unified policy: burial places must be treated with **permanence, reverence, and due process**.

- **Abandoned cemetery statutes (La. R.S. 8:411 - 418)** prevent neglect and ensure oversight.
- **Abandoned interment space statutes (8:308)** prevent waste and allow re-use within active cemeteries.
- **Dedication-removal statutes (La. R.S. 8:306–307)** protect the sanctity of entire cemeteries by requiring court supervision.

Together, they ensure that no portion of a cemetery — individual or entire — may be repurposed or disturbed without legal authority, proper notice, and respect for the dead.

Role of the Cemetery Authority

A Cemetery Authority should:

- Maintain complete and accurate ownership and interment records;
- Inspect and document cemetery conditions regularly;
- Communicate with the **Louisiana Cemetery Board** regarding any potential abandonment (**La. R.S. 8:66**);
- Notify families or known owners of deterioration or safety hazards;
- Apply for an **abandoned cemetery sales and management license** when ownership cannot be located; and
- Seek judicial relief for dedication removal only when all preservation measures are exhausted.

Conclusion

Louisiana law draws clear lines between **abandoned cemeteries, abandoned interment spaces**, and **removal of dedication.**

- **La. R.S. 8:411 – 418** governs cemeteries that have lost identifiable ownership.
- **La. R.S. 8:308** governs individual unused or abandoned spaces.
- **La. R.S. 8:306 – 307** governs the formal removal of dedication of cemetery land.

Together, these provisions protect the sacred trust inherent in cemetery property—ensuring that neither neglect, disuse, nor convenience can erase the respect owed to the dead. Cemetery Authorities must approach all such matters with prudence, compassion, and fidelity to both civil law and moral duty.

CHAPTER 16

CEMETERIES AND CULTURAL PRESERVATION

Cemeteries in Louisiana are more than places of burial; they are cultural landmarks that preserve the memories, identities, and heritages of entire communities. From the iconic above-ground tombs of New Orleans to rural parish graveyards and small family plots, these sacred spaces embody centuries of faith, struggle, and tradition. Recognizing their significance, the Louisiana Legislature has enacted statutory protections for historic cemeteries, ensuring their preservation for future generations.

Definition of Historic Cemeteries

La. R.S. 8:903 defines a cemetery as "historic" if it is at least **fifty years old.** This broad definition encompasses not only famous cemeteries in New Orleans and Baton Rouge, but also numerous small churchyards, African American burial grounds, Native American sites, and community cemeteries across the state.

The statute acknowledges that many historic cemeteries may no longer be active but remain vital as cultural and historical resources.

Protections Afforded by Law

Historic cemeteries are subject to enhanced protections under **La. R.S. 8:903 - 910**. These include:

1. **Preservation Mandate** – Cemetery Authorities and local governments must protect historic cemeteries against destruction, neglect, or inappropriate development.
2. **Restrictions on Removal or Alteration** – Historic cemeteries may not be altered, abandoned, or removed without compliance with statutory procedures and court approval.
3. **Coordination with Historic Preservation Agencies** – Preservation efforts may involve the Louisiana Division of Archaeology, the State Historic Preservation Office, and local preservation groups.

These statutory provisions affirm that cemeteries are part of Louisiana's cultural patrimony, not merely private burial places.

Community and Cultural Significance

Louisiana's cultural mosaic is reflected in its cemeteries.

- **Catholic Cemeteries** embody the Church's central role in community life.
- **African American Cemeteries often trace their roots to Reconstruction-**era communities, preserving the legacy of freedom and resilience.
- **Native American Burial Grounds** are tangible links to ancient cultures and deserve respectful protection.
- **Fraternal and Benevolent Society Cemeteries** illustrate the role of mutual aid in immigrant and working-class communities.

Cultural preservation ensures these diverse stories are not erased by neglect or urban development.

DUTIES OF THE CEMETERY AUTHORITY

Cemetery Authorities with responsibility for historic cemeteries must:

- Maintain and protect grounds consistent with perpetual care obligations **(La. R.S. 8:454 - 466)**.
- Avoid removal of dedication except in strict compliance with **La. R.S. 8:308.**
- Work with preservation agencies and historical commissions to obtain support and funding.
- Preserve records and genealogical data associated with the Cemetery.

Failure to maintain historic cemeteries may expose Cemetery Authorities to oversight by the Louisiana Cemetery Board **(La. R.S. 8:66)** and public action by families and community groups.

Public Policy Considerations

The preservation of historic cemeteries reflects Louisiana's dual commitment to religious faith and cultural identity. Protecting these places safeguards the dignity of the dead and preserves the living memory of the communities they served.

By codifying protections for historic cemeteries, Louisiana law ensures that future generations will continue to encounter their history not only in books and archives, but also in the sacred spaces where their ancestors are buried.

Conclusion

Historic cemeteries are monuments to Louisiana's past. Through **La. R.S. 8:903 – 910**, the Legislature has affirmed their significance and placed stewardship duties upon Cemetery Authorities and local communities. By honoring these obligations, Cemetery Authorities fulfill a sacred trust, ensuring that the legacy of Louisiana's people endures in the very ground where they are laid to rest.

CHAPTER 17

PET INTERMENTS UNDER LOUISIANA CEMETERY LAW

Although Title 8 of the Louisiana Revised Statutes is primarily concerned with the interment of human remains, the Legislature has also made provision for the burial of pets within certain cemeteries. This accommodation acknowledges the emotional bond families share with their companion animals, while ensuring that cemeteries maintain their dignity and comply with public health standards.

STATUTORY BASIS

Louisiana now expressly permits the interment of **cremated pet remains** in limited circumstances under **La. R.S. 8:907**. The 2023 act was both enacted in **La. R.S. 8:907** and amended **La. R.S. 8:1(7)** to clarify that, to the extent allowed by Title 8, a "cemetery" may include places used for the interment of pet remains.

Core Requirements

To lawfully include pet remains, **all** of the following must be met:

1. **Dedicated area with no prior human interments.** The cemetery space must be located in a cemetery – or in a specifically designated section – where no human remains have previously been interred. That area must be formally dedicated (or amended) by the Cemetery Authority with an official act of dedication filed in accordance with **La. R.S. 8:304(B)**.
2. **"Incidental" to human interment.** Pet interment must be **incidental to human interment**, which can occur before, at the same time, or after the pet interment.
3. **Written authorization.** Written authorization from the owner of the Cemetery space or a person with the right of interment, as outlined in the Cemetery's adopted rules, is required. (The cemetery has **no duty** to investigate who owns the pet remains.)
4. **Rules indicate cremation only.** The use must comply with the cemetery's rules; pet remains must be **cremated**, kept in a **closed receptacle**, and placed in a **grave, vault, crypt, or niche**. A cemetery may limit the **types of pets** and **pet interments** and must provide a **list of charges**.
5. **Discretion preserved.** No cemetery is **required** to allow pet interments; **La. R.S. 8:907** preserves the Cemetery Authority's discretion and also clarifies **no liability** for permitting or not permitting in a cemetery not dedicated to pet remains. **Preexisting contracts** are not altered.

Practical Policy Notes

- **Religious/mission alignment.** Catholic and other faith-based cemeteries can maintain human-only sections and decline pet interments entirely; **La. R.S. 8:907** is permissive, not mandatory. This is an important distinction because the statute recognizes the rights of religious institutions to restrict burial to human remains only.

- **Paper trail matters.** The act of dedication (or amendment) for any pet-eligible section must be **filed with the parish clerk and the Louisiana Cemetery Board** under **La. R.S. 8:304(B)**; the LCB's guidance materials likewise point operators to **La. R.S. 8:1(7) and La. R.S. 8:907** when dedicating such sections.

COMPLIANCE CHECKLIST

- ✓ Confirm **policy stance** (permit or prohibit) and adopt/refresh written **rules & regulations** referencing **La. R.S. 8:907**.
- ✓ If permitted, dedicate a new section (with no prior human interments) or amend an existing dedication; file as per **La. R.S. 8:304(B)** (parish clerk and Louisiana Cemetery Board). Update maps/plats.
- ✓ Create an **authorization form** for the owner/right-holder to sign (pet cremation, receptacle, placement location, fee schedule).
- ✓ Verify **cremation** and **closed receptacle**; record interment in the Cemetery's permanent records and space card.
- ✓ Publish and maintain **approved charges**. If limiting pet types or interment modes, state these limits in writing.
- ✓ Add **contract disclosures** and signage that clarify pet interments are allowed only in the designated section(s).

Conclusion

The introduction of **La. R.S. 8:907** represents a thoughtful modernization of Louisiana's cemetery law, balancing tradition, compassion, and regulation. While the statute allows families to memorialize beloved pets alongside human interments, it does so within a defined legal and ethical framework that protects the integrity of all cemeteries.

For Cemetery Authorities, this development emphasizes the importance of precision in policy — each decision regarding pet interment must align with statutory requirements and the Cemetery's mission.

Ultimately, **La. R.S. 8:907** affirms that cemeteries may accommodate modern expressions of remembrance without compromising dignity, order, or religious principle. Whether permitted or prohibited, every interment must be handled with integrity and care.

GRAVE MATTERS
Personal Reflections
of a Cemetery Director

THE GRAVE AND MAN'S BEST FRIEND

I've heard the phrase more than a few times: *"I brought the cremated remains of Mom's pet Fluffy because she wanted to be buried with her."*

As noted earlier, Louisiana law **does not prohibit** the burial of animal remains, provided certain conditions are met. **La. R.S. Title 8** and the accompanying administrative regulations give **cemeteries broad discretion** in determining what may or may not be interred within their grounds. The law distinguishes between *what is permitted* under state regulation and *what is permitted under the cemetery's internal governance*. In other words, while the state allows cemeteries to include pet remains if they choose to do so, **no cemetery is required** to do so.

This distinction is critical. Each cemetery – public, private, religious, or fraternal – establishes its own **rules of operation, dedication, and use**. These rules are not merely administrative conveniences; they reflect the **identity and mission** of the cemetery itself. For instance, **Catholic cemeteries**, such as the one I oversee, are **consecrated grounds** dedicated to the burial of **human persons** who share in the hope of resurrection. Our faith attributes a particular dignity to the human body – even in death – as the visible sign of a person created in the image of God. That dignity, which finds its ultimate meaning in the Incarnation and Resurrection, is unique to humanity.

Thus, Catholic cemeteries do not allow the interment of pets or animal remains within consecrated space. This is not because we deny the goodness, affection, or companionship of animals – far from it. Anyone who has loved a family pet knows the profound emotional bonds they bring and the comfort they offer in life's most difficult moments. Instead, the restriction reflects **theological**

boundaries, not emotional ones. It is about maintaining the sacred character of the ground that has been blessed and set apart exclusively for human burial.

That said, **civil cemeteries** and **nonsectarian burial grounds** are entirely within their rights to establish different rules. Many privately operated cemeteries, particularly those not under ecclesiastical jurisdiction, have designated **sections for pet burials** or **combined human and pet memorials**. Some allow cremated animal remains to be placed discreetly within a family member's grave or niche, while others maintain separate "companion sections" for both. These practices are consistent with Louisiana law, provided the cemetery's governing authority has approved them and the dedication of the land includes such uses.

Ultimately, the question of whether pets may be buried in a cemetery is not a legal mandate but a **matter of policy and purpose**. Each cemetery's board or authority must determine whether such burials align with its founding mission, religious identity, and the expectations of the families it serves.

For Catholic cemeteries, the answer remains clear: **our sacred ground is reserved for those who share in the promise of resurrection.** Yet even as we hold that conviction, we recognize the deep affection people feel for their animals. Their love, loyalty, and presence often reflect, in small but meaningful ways, the love of God that we experience in one another.

To that extent, even when pets cannot share the same resting place, they remain part of the same story – one of love, memory, and gratitude for the creatures who walked with us through life.

CONCLUSION

Cemeteries in Louisiana are more than burial grounds – they are living testaments to faith, heritage, and the enduring bonds of family. They are places where the law intersects with culture, where statutes guide practice, and where the sacred duty of burying the dead assumes both spiritual and civic significance. Title 8 of the Louisiana Revised Statutes, as explored throughout this handbook, establishes a framework that ensures cemeteries are not merely maintained, but protected, respected, and entrusted to the care of future generations.

THE ROLE OF THE CEMETERY AUTHORITY

As a Cemetery Authority, your responsibilities extend far beyond record-keeping and grounds maintenance. You serve in a dual capacity: steward of sacred ground and fiduciary of public trust. On the one hand, you must comfort grieving families while honoring traditions and religious practices with sensitivity. On the other hand, you must comply with the strict provisions of law – managing trust funds, issuing contracts, regulating interments, and working in partnership with the Louisiana Cemetery Board. These two roles are not opposed but complementary, each reinforcing the dignity and order that cemeteries represent.

This handbook has sought to equip you with both the technical understanding of the law and the practical tools necessary to apply it effectively. From the distinction between interment rights and land ownership to the establishment of perpetual care funds and the protocols for disinterment and reinterment, each chapter underscores that compliance is not merely a legal obligation—it is also an act of respect toward families and the deceased.

Framework as Safeguard

Louisiana's civil law tradition sets its cemeteries apart from those in other states. Here, interment rights are recognized as servitudes, not fee simple property interests. This unique structure requires constant clarity in contracts, transfers, and succession matters. Families must understand that they are not purchasing land, but rather acquiring a right of burial, which is protected and regulated by statute. By maintaining accurate records and following Title 8 provisions, Cemetery Authorities prevent disputes, avoid costly errors, and preserve public trust.

The law also provides the necessary safeguards for families – ensuring that perpetual care funds are properly managed, that disinterments cannot occur without proper consent or court order, and that rules and regulations are applied fairly and reasonably. These protections are not burdensome restrictions; rather, they are the guardrails that allow cemeteries to remain sacred, stable, and trustworthy institutions.

Cultural and Spiritual Dimensions

Beyond the law, cemeteries occupy a special place in Louisiana's cultural and religious life. From the above-ground tombs of New Orleans to the rural resting places of Acadiana, cemeteries embody history, tradition, and faith. Annual observances, such as All Saints' Day, highlight how cemeteries are not only places of mourning but also of community, memory, and renewal.

The work of Cemetery Authorities must therefore be guided by more than statutes – it must also be rooted in respect for the traditions that families bring to these spaces. By striking a balance between statutory compliance and pastoral sensitivity, you ensure that cemeteries remain places where faith and culture can continue to flourish.

Fiduciary Responsibility

Equally important is the fiduciary dimension of your role. Trust funds – whether for perpetual care or merchandise – are not optional or symbolic; they are legal obligations that guarantee the long-term preservation of sacred grounds. Mismanagement of these funds not only violates the law but also erodes the confidence of the families who have placed their trust in your cemetery. By properly managing investments, documenting deposits, and filing required reports, Cemetery Authorities fulfill their fiduciary duty and safeguard the legacy of their institutions.

The Continuing Work of Stewardship

The stewardship of cemeteries does not end with compliance. It is a continuing mission to preserve order, dignity, and sacredness in places that hold deep meaning for families and communities. Errors may occur – such as double sales or incomplete documentation – but Title 8 provides mechanisms to correct them. Disputes may arise among heirs, but the law provides processes for their resolution. At each juncture, your role is to apply the law with fairness, transparency, and compassion, remembering that behind every transaction is a family seeking peace of mind.

Closing Thoughts

This handbook is not intended to replace the advice of legal counsel, nor does it provide all the answers for every situation that may arise. Each cemetery, each family, and each case presents unique challenges. Whenever there is uncertainty, you are strongly advised to consult a qualified attorney familiar with Louisiana cemetery law. By doing so, you ensure that your actions remain not only pastoral and practical but also legally sound.

This handbook was born out of my own journey as the Executive Director of a Cemetery, where I found that there were no resources beyond simply searching through all of Title 8. I hope this book serves as a reliable resource for you when you have questions and need a quick answer. The goal here was not to replace Title 8, but rather to create a go-to book where you can quickly find answers based on the topic you need.

Ultimately, burying the dead is one of humanity's oldest acts of mercy. In Louisiana, it is also a carefully regulated legal duty. By mastering the provisions of Title 8 and applying them with integrity, you honor both the law and the sacred trust entrusted to you. In so doing, you ensure that cemeteries remain what they are meant to be: places of dignity, reverence, and perpetual care.

May your stewardship of sacred grounds always reflect compassion and justice, and may your works safeguard not only the resting places of the departed, but also the trust of the living.

GRAVE MATTERS
Personal Reflections of a Cemetery Director

CUSTODIANS OF THE UNDERGROUND CITY

As I come to the close of this work, I am reminded that the ministry of **cemetery management** is not merely about **grounds, records, and rules**—it is about **souls, stories, and stewardship.** Every space we tend, every family we serve, and every decision we make is part of something **far deeper than administration.** It is, at its heart, a **work of mercy.**

We walk daily among reminders of **mortality and mystery.** The monuments we pass and the names we read whisper the same truth that has echoed through the ages: *we are dust, and to dust we shall return.* Yet in that truth lies not despair, but a profound **sense of peace and purpose.** The work of the cemetery is not about death – it is about **faith, memory, and the hope that lives on.** It reminds us that **love endures**, and that those who have gone before us remain part of a **larger communion of saints** that transcends time.

To those who serve in this ministry, the cemetery is more than sacred ground—it is **a classroom of humility.** It teaches that perfection lies not in control but in **care**, not in grandeur but in **grace.** We learn that weeds will grow back, headstones will weather, and families will grieve in their own ways. But we also learn that **gentle consistency, honest communication**, and **quiet compassion** accomplish more than any grand policy ever could.

Our **rules and records** matter deeply—not as bureaucratic instruments, but as **guardrails for justice and memory.** They ensure that the **common good** is respected, that the **trust of families** is protected, and that the **dignity of the dead** remains undisturbed. The order we preserve is not a restriction—it is an act of reverence. By enforcing rules fairly and maintaining consistency, we build confidence in something eternal: the idea that sacred ground must remain sacred for all.

The cemetery is also a mirror of our **shared humanity**. Within its walls lie the famous and the forgotten, the wealthy and the poor, the saint and the sinner—all resting side by side. The grass does not grow differently over one than another. In this silent equality, we are reminded that every human life carries **inherent dignity**, and that a common truth binds our final resting places: **death unites what life divides.**

It is a humbling thing to care for the dead. In tending to the places where others can no longer speak for themselves, we become **keepers of memory** and **guardians of peace.** The beauty of a well-kept cemetery is not found in its lawns or marble, but in the **love, discipline, and devotion** those details represent. Each act of maintenance, each record preserved, each flower placed is a small testament to **faithfulness in the unseen**.

And yet, for those who serve in this ministry, the reward is not a plaque or a paycheck—it is the quiet satisfaction of knowing that **something sacred has been preserved.** We plant grass that others will walk upon. We restore monuments that others will visit. We write names in ledgers that will outlast our own. This is the hidden holiness of our calling: to work not for recognition, but for **continuity**, ensuring that those entrusted to us are **never forgotten.**

As you close this book, I invite you to reflect not only on the laws and logistics of cemetery management, but also on the grace that accompanies this work. May we continue to serve faithfully, to comfort those who mourn, and to uphold the **sacred trust** placed in our hands.

For in the quiet of every cemetery, beneath the marble and the moss, **heaven and earth meet**—and we are given the holy task of **caring for both.**

TABLE OF STATUTES CITED

Other Statutes and Codes

GLOSSARY OF TERMS

Abandonment of Cemetery Property –
The condition in which a cemetery or portion of cemetery land has ceased to be maintained, visited, or used for interment purposes, under **La. R.S. 8:308 - 312**, a court may declare a cemetery abandoned and authorize the removal of dedication and relocation of human remains.

Access (Visitation Rights) –
The legal right of family members and descendants to visit and maintain gravesites is recognized as a servitude of passage in favor of the relatives of the deceased (**La. R.S. 8:304; 8:803**; see also **La. Civ. Code arts. 646–647**).

Affidavit of Heirship –
A sworn statement identifying the lawful heirs or successors of a deceased interment-right holder. It serves as evidence for the transfer or recognition of burial rights under **La. R.S. 8:803 - 805** and related succession law. Not to be confused with an OMV form by the same name.

Authentic Act (and the Cemetery Exception) –
In Louisiana civil law, an *authentic act* is a written instrument executed before a notary public and two witnesses (*La. Civ. Code art. 1833*), serving as full proof of its contents. Cemetery conveyances, however, are expressly **exempt** from the authentic-act requirement by **La. R.S. 8:603**; a private written instrument signed by the parties is sufficient to transfer interment rights.

Burial Permit –
An official authorization for interment issued pursuant to the state's vital records laws **(La. R.S. 40:50 et seq.)**. Cemeteries are required to retain burial permits in their permanent records for inspection by the Louisiana Cemetery Board.

Cemetery Authority –
Any person, partnership, corporation, association, or religious entity owning or operating a cemetery in Louisiana, as defined in **La. R.S. 8:1(6)**. The authority bears fiduciary and statutory responsibility for the operation, care, and recordkeeping of the cemetery.

Cemetery Board, Louisiana (LCB) –
The regulatory agency created under **La. R.S. 8:61 - 67** to supervise and license cemetery authorities, enforce trust-fund compliance, and adopt reasonable rules for the industry.

Columbarium –
A structure or room containing niches for the inurnment of cremated remains. Construction and development timelines are governed by **La. R.S. 8:606**.

Dedication of Land –
The formal act by which property is devoted exclusively to cemetery purposes, creating a perpetual servitude of use. Once dedicated under **La. R.S. 8:304**, the land cannot be used for any other purpose without a court-ordered removal of dedication.

Dation en Paiement –
A civil-law transaction whereby property is transferred to a creditor in satisfaction of a debt. In cemetery practice, it may be used to transfer interment rights in exchange for cancellation of a purchase obligation.

Disinterment / Reinterment –
The lawful removal of human remains from their place of interment, followed—if applicable—by reburial elsewhere. Governed by **La. R.S. 8:659 - 661**, requiring consent of next of kin or judicial authorization.

Error Correction (Double Sale or Wrong Burial) –
The statutory authority of a cemetery to correct errors in interment or conveyance under **La. R.S. 8:708**, allowing relocation or reassignment with due notice to families.

Fiduciary Duty –
The obligation of a cemetery authority, officer, or trustee to manage perpetual-care and merchandise trust funds in good faith and in the best interest of lot owners and the public. See **La. R.S. 8:454; 8:601 - 606**.

Interment –
The act or process of placing human remains in a grave, tomb, vault, mausoleum, or niche.

Interment Right –
A personal servitude of use granting the holder the right to bury human remains in a designated space. It is heritable and transferable under **La. R.S. 8:803 - 805,** but does not convey ownership of land.

Merchandise Trust Fund –
A trust established under **La. R.S. 8:601 - 606** to secure payments received for merchandise or services to be delivered in the future (such as vaults, markers, or pre-need contracts). Funds are deposited with a qualified trustee to ensure performance.

Particular Care (Special Care) –
Funds established for the maintenance of a specific burial space or section of a cemetery, separate from the general perpetual-care trust. Defined in *La. R.S. 8:454(B).*

Perpetual Care –
The general and permanent trust fund created for the upkeep, repair, and embellishment of cemetery grounds, structures, and improvements, established under **La. R.S. 8:454 - 466** and subject to the supervision of the LCB.

Personal Servitude –
A limited real right conferring use or enjoyment of property belonging to another. Interment rights are classified as personal servitudes of use under **La. Civ. Code arts. 534–645**.

Removal of Dedication –
The judicial process by which land once dedicated for cemetery purposes may, after compliance with **La. R.S. 8:308 - 312**, be released from that use. All remains must first be lawfully disinterred and reinterred elsewhere.

Rules and Regulations (Cemetery) –
Reasonable and published operational policies governing interments, memorials, access, and conduct within the cemetery, authorized by **La. R.S. 8:303 - 305**.

Servitude of Burial (Right of Interment) –
A personal servitude arising from dedication that allows the use of cemetery land for interment. This right continues even after ownership of the land changes, until dedication is lawfully removed.

Successor / Heir –
A person who inherits or otherwise lawfully acquires interment rights upon the death of the original holder, determined under **La. R.S. 8:805** and Louisiana succession law.

Testamentary Trust (for Burial Space) –
A trust created within a will to designate future interments or manage burial spaces. It may preserve inalienable family burial rights under **La. R.S. 8:805**.

Trustee –
A state- or federally-chartered financial institution authorized to administer cemetery trust funds, subject to examination by the Louisiana Cemetery Board.

Undeveloped Cemetery Land –
Land acquired for future expansion but not yet platted, improved, or dedicated for cemetery purposes. Once interment spaces are sold, development obligations attach under **La. R.S. 8:304 - 308.**

Usufruct-like Burial Right of Spouse –
A surviving spouse's right to continued use of an interment space held in the name of the deceased spouse, analogous to a usufruct under **La. Civ. Code art. 549** and recognized in **La. R.S. 8:805.**

Waiver of Interment Right –
A written and notarized declaration relinquishing one's right to be interred in a particular space, governed by **La. R.S. 8:809 - 810.**

Westlawn Cemeteries v. Louisiana Cemetery Board (2022) –
A Louisiana First Circuit decision clarifying limits on the Board's regulatory power over perpetual-care fund distributions, reaffirming the statutory autonomy of cemetery authorities.

GENERAL INDEX

A

B

C

D

E

F

G

H

I

J

L

M

N

O

P

R

S

T

U

V

W

WEB RESOURCES

The following online resources provide direct access to Louisiana cemetery law, regulatory agencies, and related guidance. These sites were referenced or relied upon in preparing this handbook:

- **The Louisiana Cemetery Handbook**
  Official website for this Handbook and the Forms Book
  https://LaCemeteryBook.com

- **Louisiana Revised Statutes, Title 8 (Cemeteries)**
  Official compilation of Louisiana cemetery laws.
  https://www.legis.la.gov/legis/Laws_Toc.aspx?folder=82&title=8

- **Louisiana Cemetery Board**
  The regulatory body overseeing cemeteries in Louisiana provides rules, compliance materials, and forms.
  https://lcb.la.gov

- **Louisiana Legislature – Laws and Codes**
  Access to all Louisiana statutes, including Title 8.
  https://www.legis.la.gov/legis/LawSearch.aspx

- **Louisiana Department of Health – Vital Records**
  Guidance on death certificates and authorizations that may intersect with burial and disinterment procedures.
  https://ldh.la.gov/vitalrecords

- **Louisiana Attorney General Opinions**
  Opinions interpreting cemetery law and related issues.
  https://www.ag.state.la.us/Opinions

NOTES

NOTES

NOTES

NOTES

NOTES

NOTES

NOTES

Made in United States
North Haven, CT
11 November 2026

22113772R00108